Frankie Wainman Junior is one of the most successful drivers in the history of oval motorsport. Since his debut in Formula 1 stock cars in 1987 at the age of sixteen, he has won more than 1,000 races including 275 finals. He is the only driver to have won the premier title in three different countries: the UK World Final, New Zealand World 240 Championship and Dutch World Cup, each of which he has won three times. He is also a thirteen-time National Points Champion and nine-time British Champion. Frankie lives in Silsden, West Yorkshire with his wife Samantha and two children, Phoebe and Frankie, both of whom also race stock cars.

FRANKIE WAINMAN JUNIOR

FWJ

My Life In Formula 1 Stock Cars

Chequered Flag
PUBLISHING

First published in the UK by Chequered Flag Publishing 2017
PO Box 4669, Sheffield, S6 9ET
www.chequeredflagpublishing.co.uk

A CIP record for this book is available from the British Library

Printed in the EU by Print Group Sp. z o.o.

ISBN 978-1-9997774-0-1

Photo credits:
Dave Bastock, p.254, front cover
Colin Casserley p.i (opp), 148, 178, 188, 224, 240, 248, back cover
Martin Fitzgerald p.170, 204
Mike Greenwood p.20, 32, 44, 54, 66, 88, 96, 104, 118, 126, 156
Paul Tully p.140, 240
Howard Turner: p.214
Frankie Wainman Junior p.iv, 10

For the fans who have followed three generations
of Wainman Racing.

Dedicated to the memory of Ben Turner.

Twenty-six silver roofs
and thirteen gold roofs between us!

FOREWORD

by Rob Speak

Many people who read this book will hear the names Rob Speak and Frankie Wainman Junior and think of one thing – that Wimbledon meeting where we both left with damaged cars, though not as damaged as the Wimbledon fence! Although me and Frankie had plenty of crashes, we also have a long history that goes back further than many people realise.

My dad used to go and watch Frankie Wainman race Formula 1 stock cars. When I got into racing Ministox there was another Frankie Wainman racing – the son of the guy my dad used to go and watch. Young Frankie was a big name already and a year older than me, and I sort of looked up to him right from the start. We had some good times together.

A couple of years after Ministox was over, I was racing my Formula 2 at Hartlepool. Frankie came into the pits with his Formula 1 but couldn't race because he was banned. I think the person who was going to drive his car didn't turn up, so Frankie happened to say to me, 'Do you fancy having a drive? You can have a go if you want.' So I spent the meeting jumping in and out of my Formula 2 and his Formula 1 and really enjoyed it, although I don't think I did anything special. We didn't particularly keep in touch with each other over the next few years. We both did a lot of meetings in the different formula we raced in and we'd have a chat if we came across each other in the pits, but that was about it.

Then, about nine years later, I got fed up with Formula 2 and some sponsors offered me the chance to drive in Formula 1, and I decided to give it a proper go. Everybody was saying that although I was the top man in Formula 2, I wouldn't have it my own way in Formula 1 – I wouldn't be any good, in other words. But I wanted to win instantly. So I had to come out all guns blazing to try to prove myself. The way I saw it was that if I went out and buried Frankie Wainman Junior and Andy Smith, the two top people at the time, everybody else would leave me alone.

It worked to a fashion, but I don't think Frankie appreciated it, and so the rivalry between Wainman and Speak was born! We both want to be the best, that's all it was. It's not that we didn't get on. It's just when you get two people who both want to be at the top of their game, they're going to clash. I had a rough first year, but after that it was really down to me, Frankie and Andy. We were a similar age and we all wanted to win. It must have been good for the fans at the time.

I had another ten years or so off and came back into Formula 1 again. I had nothing to prove, I'd already been World Champion and had been at the top of the sport, but this time I was expected to do well. I hadn't been watching any racing while I was away, I had been completely out of it, but I quickly found out that Frankie wasn't the same as when I left. He wasn't as quick and dominant as he had been. I knew he'd had a bad crash at Hednesford – did that put him back a little bit? But then I came back into it and he seemed to raise his game a little bit. Maybe it breathed new life into him?

However much we have competed against each other and however much we have been rivals, it's always been about the racing on the track. We have a huge amount of respect for each other. We knocked each other about on the track, but if one of us was having a problem off the track – on the road or something like that – we'd stop to make sure that the other was alright. That's the way it should be.

Now I've stopped racing again and moved into promoting at Skegness. Can I ever imagine Frankie stopping racing? Not at all. It's his life. He puts everything into racing. I can honestly say that I couldn't make the sacrifices that Frankie does – it's not that important to me. But to him, it's everything. The sacrifices he has made over the years to go racing are second to none. In fact, that sums Frankie up pretty well, really. Second to none.

My training wheels!

1

I decide I'm going to make my move on the last bend. That seems like the best way to win the World Final.

I'm in second place, only one car in front of me. I follow that familiar car round. Blue bumper, orange boot, red roof. Number 212. The only person between me and glory is my own dad.

Bouncing around the bumpy track, it takes all my concentration and skill to close the gap. Dad certainly has more power under his right foot, so I need to squeeze everything out of my own car. Slowly but surely, the gap between us is reduced. I'm being pelted by the dirt from his tyres, but nothing is going to put me off.

I work out what I'm going to do in the run up to the last bend. No need to touch him, just use the better traction I have. I let him drift wide and sneak up the inside, willing *my car to go faster. He looms in my mirror but can't get past before the finish line. I've done it!*

I'm the 1979 Formula 1 Stock Car World Champion. And I'm only eight years old.

The history books record that the 1979 World Final was won by number 212, my dad, Frankie Wainman. It was raced at White City in Manchester on Saturday 29 September. The World Final that I won was actually the product of my overactive imagination. I did beat my dad fair and square, but we were only racing around a field on the farm where we lived. Dad was racing his World Final winner, I was racing a stock car he'd bought for me.

My car was built by Derek Green, a local F1 driver and a friend of my dad, but it was crap and would never have done as a proper stock car. My dad bought it from him and put in a diesel engine that he had lying around the place. It was painted up in the same colour scheme as he used on his cars – blue chassis, orange body, red roof – colours which, at the time, were instantly recognisable as belonging to my dad.

I also had the same name as my dad. My name, as I'm sure you know, is Frank Wainman. Frank Gordon Michael Wainman, to be exact. My middle names came from my mum's side of the family, named after her dad and brother. My first name... well, I certainly wasn't the first Frank Wainman. My dad was called Frank too, so was my grandad, so was his dad. I think that I was about the fifth generation to be called Frank. So I suppose I should really have Frankie Wainman Junior Junior Junior Junior Junior on my cars!

I was born in October 1971 into a stock car family, although it hadn't been for long. My dad had only started racing a year before. I think he went to Nelson to watch a few meetings and decided that he could build a car just as good as the ones that he saw racing. The first one he built was pretty good for its day, it was a Morris LD van chassis with a twin-cam six-cylinder Jaguar engine. It might not have been the best looking car but there were plenty of ugly tanks around at the time.

I was ten days old when I went to my first meeting, not that I can remember anything about it. It was a meeting at Coventry and my dad's only finish was fifth in the consolation, although considering that he was only a yellow top at the time, perhaps that's only to be expected.

My dad must have been twenty-three when he first started in stock cars, so he was a little older than I was when he first started, but we both learned to drive in a similar way. Growing up on a farm, we have both driven tractors all our lives. I think that's a big part of our success. Like him, I was driving tractors from when I was a small child. I'd sit on my grandad's knee while he was in the fields, gradually learning what the various levers and pedals did. By the time I was four or five, I could manoeuvre some of the tractors better than the people who brought the bales of hay in from the fields! I was reversing the tractors with trailers attached. I was the only one confident enough to get into top gear and I was tiny, barely able to reach the pedals. My dad was the same.

Growing up on a farm meant that I had plenty of space to roam and get into scrapes when I was a child. Even then, it often involved cars. One time, when I was about four or five, I went into the garage where my dad kept his stock car. I put some wooden planks over the inspection pit where he worked underneath his car. Then I sat on my little plastic ride-on car and lined myself up with the boards. I'd push myself towards the pit, accelerating as much as possible, and lift my legs in the air as I went over the planks. It was great fun – until my mum found out what I was doing and banned me! It's probably a good job she did. Who knows what would have happened if I'd missed the planks and tumbled into the pit?

Another time I followed my dad into the garage when he was doing some joinery. I was always in there with him, watching him and following him around. I borrowed one of his hammers and a saw – I say borrowed, but I never asked – and decided to saw a plank of wood, just like I saw him doing. The only trouble was that the plank of wood I sawed was on top of a big, fat electric cable. I was wearing a pair of red wellies. I loved those wellies, I wouldn't take them off, even in the middle of summer. On this occasion it's lucky I was wearing them because there was an almighty bang and the electrics all went out. The rubber in them stopped me from getting a big electric shock, although it didn't stop my mum going mental again. I think I was bought a toy tool set after that, although it wasn't the same!

Most of the time I followed my dad around the garage, he was working on his stock car. The racing bug had bitten him badly. We went to as many meetings as possible as I grew up. My mum was quite strict and wouldn't let me have many days off school. There were midweek meetings and I'd still manage to get to them. We'd have to leave straight after school finished and drive to places like Skegness, but the rule was I still had to go to school on the next day no matter what time we got home, even if it was two or three o'clock in the morning.

Everybody thinks of my dad as one of the stars of the seventies, but it actually took him a while to get there. He didn't win his first race until 1972 and didn't win a final until the end of 1973. But by the time superstar grade was introduced, for the start of 1976, he was up there with the best. He was one of the original six superstars, with Dave Chisholm, Mike Close, Doug Cronshaw, Willie Harrison and Stuart Smith. That's quite a list – if you chose the top ten drivers in the history of the sport, it's quite possible all six would feature in it.

Stuart Smith was at the height of his career right through the seventies, he was winning the National Points title easily each year. It was a doddle for him, mainly because his equipment was far better than everybody else's. Having said that, there's no doubt he was a really skilled driver – if he was racing now he'd still be doing well. But it would be interesting to see what would have happened if Stuart had been driving in my dad's cars and my dad got to race in his – or if Stuart swapped with somebody like Willie Harrison, Brian Powles or Dave Hodgson – would he have won so many titles then?

To be honest, I don't have any memories of those early years of my dad's racing career. I wasn't bothered about watching him race – I was more bothered about messing around in the pits with the other kids. My three big mates were Andy Smith, Andy Hodgson and Stevie Hodgson. I grew up with them. I couldn't wait to see them each time we drove to a meeting and we often used to stop at each other's houses afterwards.

Even though we weren't interested in the racing all that much, stock cars certainly helped me grow up. We were surrounded by family and friends every weekend. Even if we disappeared for the duration of the meeting and our parents didn't see us, there were plenty of people around who knew us. Everybody kept an eye on the little ones to make sure we were safe and not getting up to any bother. Then, as we all grew up and gradually started to take an interest in the cars and the racing, it gave us a hobby that kept us busy. Once I was old enough to realise that messing around with the cars was more fun than jumping in muddy puddles, I was in the garage as often as possible. As soon as I got home from school I was in there, and every weekend when we weren't racing.

Living in the middle of rural West Yorkshire, as we do up here, you don't get kids hanging about on street corners. I happen to think that's a good thing. Stock cars gave me a focus in my life. I can see how easily some kids get into trouble when they don't have anything they are interested in. They go out and cause trouble just because they are bored. We've had a few kids from the village who were getting into trouble come up to our farm to see if they could find a hobby. Often it was borderline whether the authorities were going to get involved with them and take them away from home. In later years, we had a troubled kid speak to my dad and ask if he could help out Danny when he was racing his Ministox. Doing something productive squared him right up. He enjoyed coming here and going racing with Danny. It gave him a focus and kept him out of trouble. There's a great saying in New Zealand – a kid in sport won't end up in court – and there's something in that.

My dad had built a little go-kart stock car for me and my sister – on one side it had Stephanie's name written on it, on the other it had mine. Then, around the time when I first started showing an interest in stock cars, when I was seven or eight years old, my dad unveiled a grand Christmas present – a proper stock car for me. It had a diesel engine in that my dad had taken from a tractor or something, so it didn't go too fast and I couldn't do too much damage, but I was still able to drive around a track that I set out in a field. Can you imagine being that young and driving a stock car? Don't get me wrong, it wasn't a Chevy or anything, but it was rear-wheel drive and it was pretty nippy. My dad used to join me with his Formula 1 car and we'd mess about and race each other, but even though mine just had an old, dud engine in, it wasn't that much slower than his! It was just like driving the real thing, although when I started in Ministox my dad had to take it off me. I couldn't drive the Mini to start with because it was front-wheel drive. I was so used to messing around in my rear-wheel drive stock car in the field that I couldn't understand why the Mini didn't handle the same way!

Around the same time that my dad bought the stock car, I was also given a child-sized motorbike. I think my sister might have gone up the wall about that one – not only did I get to drive around in a stock car, I also had a motorbike. I enjoyed messing around with that too, although I always preferred four wheels to two. I decided to leave the motorbike stuff to the other motorsport family from Silsden. As well as my dad doing well in stock cars, the local paper was full of reports about Martin Lampkin, who won the first ever FIM Trials World Championship in 1975, and his older brother Arthur, who won loads of trials and motocross events. Martin's son, Dougie Lampkin, went on to win countless titles and was a star on *Junior Kick Start*, a classic television programme on the BBC in the eighties. I had to wait to get a starring role on the BBC, but it did come a few years later! Who'd have thought that the most famous family in motorbike trials and the most famous family in stock car racing would both come from the same little village? And yes, Smith fans, I really did say that the Wainmans are the most famous family in stock car racing!

Part of the reason why I turned down bikes in favour of cars was because around the time when I was choosing between them my dad had his biggest success on the track. He started the 1979 World Final on the outside of the front row. Next to him was Stuart Smith, a driver who, despite all his wins throughout the seventies, had only won two World Finals. He would have to wait before he won any more too, because my dad knocked him wide on the first bend and he dropped right back. Dad's biggest competition in that race came from Brian Powles and Bert Finnikin, but despite losing the lead to both of them, he managed to fight back and take the chequered flag.

As I watched Dad win the World Final, I made a decision. At some point in the future, I was going to win the gold roof too.

My first and last years in Ministox, in my opinion the
best place for stock car drivers to learn their craft

2

I've been racing Ministox for more than five years, but only now am I in a position to win a few races. And this one is my best win yet.

It's taken about four hours to drive up the M6 to New-tongrange, just south of Edinburgh, so I can take part in the Scottish Open Championship. Only one other lad, my main rival, has bothered to cross the border, so it's us against thirty Scottish cars. But we've shown them what English guys are made of, and I've beaten him too, taking the chequered flag and the championship title. It's one of the few championships I'll win in Ministox, so it's certainly a sweet success.

I'll make sure to rub it in to that rival of mine. His name is Rob Speak, and he'll still be a rival thirty years later!

If I was going to become a Formula 1 Stock Car World Champion like my dad, I had to start somewhere. Like many other stock car drivers, my path to F1 started in Ministox.

Given that I had already shown an interest in racing, mainly by blasting around the fields in my diesel stock car, it wasn't a surprise that I jumped at the chance to race in Ministox when I turned ten years old in 1981. My dad was certainly keen that I start racing, but he didn't really have the time or the money to put into my Minis. If he had done, it would have been at the expense of his own racing, and this was the stage when he was starting to challenge for the silver roof, so I can understand why he didn't. So it fell to my grandad to help me. He did a lot to put that first Ministox together, although it wasn't a particularly great car.

I had a lot of time for my grandad, we spent a lot of time together when I was a kid. He lived on the farm too, right next door. It's almost like I grew up with them because I'd see them every day. When I was young I'd wake up, go out of the door and in to see Grandma and Grandad to see if they had any sweets! Sometimes I'd stop with them and sleep round there. As I grew up I'd go round every morning and have a bacon sandwich with Grandma, as I got older I'd go and have a coffee with her.

It was my grandad who first started the Wainman association with Foster Cliffe Farm in Silsden. Like most men of his age, he served during the Second World War. In fact, he saw quite a lot of action – he fought with the Duke of Wellington's Regiment in Egypt and Italy and was there when Rome was taken by the Allies. After the war ended he was sent to Palestine before being demobbed home in 1946. He had married my grandma before the war, so when he came back he started to work on her family farm, but he always wanted one of his own. He had his eye on Foster Cliffe Farm but it was owned by Skipton Castle. When the opportunity arose, he got a mortgage and bought it from them in 1949.

Grandad ran this place as a dairy farm and it was pretty successful, partly because he was willing to use new technology. He was one of the first people in the area to buy a tractor and that led on to bigger and better things. Being mechanically minded, Grandad started to buy old, knackered tractors to recondition and sell on. He advertised them for sale in the local newspapers and one day two Pakistani men came to look at them – one from Burnley, one from Bradford. It turned out these two guys knew each other and, once they got talking to my grandad, they told him they were sending the tractors to their families in Pakistan. That got my grandad into the export business – he would trawl the auctions to buy old tractors, do them up and send them to Pakistan. To make sure they weren't damaged in transit, he spot-welded any loose parts to make sure they didn't break or fall off.

It snowballed really quickly because there was a good market for little tractors over there and they'd take whatever Grandad could get his hands on. By the end of the 1970s he was sending five or six a week and tractor exporting had taken over from the dairy farm, so the herd was sold. The tractor business eventually dried up after a factory was built in Pakistan, but by then my dad was making a bit of money by doing hire cars at race meetings and Grandad started to help him, so the cows never returned.

So my grandad certainly knew what he was doing with a spanner and he helped me put a Ministox together. Ministox back then were very different to Ministox now. Nobody bothered with a space frame chassis because there was no need. Old Minis weren't hard to come across, they were everywhere in the seventies and eighties, you'd even get them given to you free. You'd start with an old Mini, rip out the inside and add a bumper and roll cage. The driver's seat was still on the right side, the pedals were in the usual place. A bloke called Richard Clarkson used to come and weld for an hour or so on a Saturday because I couldn't weld back then, so I'd get everything cut and he used to weld it up. I soon learned how to weld myself so I wasn't relying on somebody else.

I remember my first race win, at Blackburn, but it probably stuck in my mind because I didn't win many others. The first problem was that I didn't go to that many meetings. Ministox didn't race very much with the F1s back then. One of the few tracks that did put them together was Long Eaton where, thanks to Keith Barber, the Minis would usually race before the F1 meeting started. But nine times out of ten we'd arrive so late that I'd miss my races because my dad was so busy helping out with the tractors or getting his hire cars ready. If I did make it to meetings, it was often without my dad at all. Quite a few meetings I was taken by Dennis Higgins – my dad looked after his son Ian's Formula 1 car, so Dennis was kind of returning the favour and helped out when he could. I was beaten by guys like Phil Woodhull, Jonathon Milicavic, Scott McKenzie and Matthew Eales. None of them were drivers who went on to do much after they finished Ministox – not in F1 anyway – but they beat me week in, week out when we were juniors.

Even though I wasn't very good, I still picked motorsport over any other sports. I had to make a decision when I was about thirteen and the school wanted to put me in the under-16 football team. I was really good at football and got picked to play for Yorkshire, but I was missing stock car meetings to play with the school. I hated it when everybody else in my family went away racing and I went to play football. I couldn't think straight. I was on the football pitch wondering what was going on in the races, whether dad's car was right, whether what I'd done in the garage was working. It came to a point where I had to decide between racing and football. Stock cars won. That was that, just one of those decisions you make in life. I could have been a really good footballer, just at the time when footballers' fame and salaries rocketed. Perhaps I'd have played in the Premiership – for Liverpool, of course – and been a multi-millionaire... Hang on a minute, can I go back and change my mind?

Only in my last year or so did things start to pick up, and that was due to one man: Martin O'Neill. Nothing to do with football this time, this Martin was a guy from Rugby who was really involved in the Ministox scene. When I first started racing, Martin was a mechanic for Keith Jones, a talented red top Ministocker who was killed in a road accident. Martin was aware of me and I think he could tell that I had a bit of potential but that I was struggling because I couldn't get to many meetings. After the tragic accident in which Keith died, Martin spoke to my dad and offered to take my car on. That's just the kind of guy that Martin (or Mon, as everybody called him) was. I wasn't the only driver he helped – after I moved on from Ministox he took Andy Smith under his wing, then Mick Sworder – not a bad threesome!

Once Martin was on board, everything changed. I started winning! Martin took me to meetings all over the country and, if he couldn't take me, arranged for somebody else to. My Ministox would usually go back to his house after a weekend's racing and Martin would get it ready for the next meeting. Sometimes he would drive me back to Silsden on a Sunday evening after a meeting, then turn round and head back down south to Rugby, arriving in the early hours and only getting a few hours of sleep before work on Monday morning. Then he'd drive back up to Silsden the next weekend to pick me up and take me to the next meeting. The hours he must have put in on the motorways were crazy, just because he wanted to help out a kid who couldn't race as often as the others.

When Martin couldn't pick me up or drop me off, I would rely on my other mechanic, Ian Frobisher. He drove me north of the border for the Scottish Open at Newtongrange. We went all the way up there in a beat-up old Ford D truck, the only other English driver who made the journey was Rob Speak. We were up against thirty Scottish drivers, but I won the race. Straight after the meeting we drove down to Skegness so I could race there the day after – but because Ian was so tired after driving all the way there, I drove the truck most of the way to Skegness while Ian slept!

Rob and I often travelled to the same meetings in my final year. We'd follow each other on the road and stop together for breaks and to have dinner. Rob's dad, Billy, was a good laugh. He'd buy Rob any decent car that came up for sale and a found a good bus to do the miles in comfort when they were on the road. As well as Rob, I used to race against Paul Harrison, although he was a couple of years older and struggled to make meetings for the same reason that I did: his dad raced F1 and that took priority. Andy Hodgson and Stevie Hodgson were also starting out – Stevie won the points championship after I had finished – and Andy Smith also raced around the same time, although he wasn't really keen until he was fourteen or fifteen, just after I left.

As well as the Scottish Open, I won the East Coast Championship in 1986 and the Northern Championship in 1986 and 1987. I never had the luck in the gold roof races – start as you mean to go on – and the silver roof didn't come my way because I retired before the end of 1987, gifting it to Rob Speak, who was younger so could race the full season. But the one race I was really keen to win was the Keith Jones Memorial, which was first raced for in 1986. We went to Skegness for that and I was really pleased when I crossed the line first. I won that for Martin O'Neill. I was only a kid, I couldn't thank him properly for helping me out, but I like to think that trophy meant a lot to him.

Racing in Ministox also helped get me more involved with my dad's Formula 1 racing. I started to help out here and there with the odd thing and by the time I was twelve years old I was really interested and keen to learn the ropes. So much so that, by the time I was fourteen, I was virtually looking after his F1 cars myself! During the three years that he won the National Points title, I was doing his car whenever I had a spare moment. It sounds odd, really. Normally F1 drivers who are fathers cut back on their own racing to help their child get more track time in Ministox. Here I was, leaving my Mini to one side to help my dad race his F1! But I certainly wasn't pushed into it. I wanted to get more involved and learn about the F1 side of racing, and my dad was so busy with the tractor business and his hire cars that his own cars were a low priority.

I'd come straight home from school, go in the garage and get straight to work. If I had homework, I'd have to do that first – I hated doing it, but if it wasn't done I couldn't work on the cars, which is what I wanted to do. Both then and now, it takes hundreds of hours to get an F1 in working order and to keep it that way. It's hard to get mechanics to give the amount of time it needs, people just don't see all the work that needs to go on behind the scenes. But I used to enjoy working on my dad's cars. It meant that I could drive them round the track on a parade lap if he won a race, although the officials stopped me from going in a mechanics race when I was fourteen because I was too young. Fair enough! Although I did persuade them to let me race later on and my record in mechanic races was pretty good – raced four, won two!

Those hours in the garage made me realise one thing – I was going to race a Formula 1 stock car as soon as I was old enough and as long as my parents let me! What I didn't realise at the time was that I was going to spend my working life in stock cars too. I did okay at school, I left

South Craven School with four O-levels, but I didn't stay on. Instead I got an apprenticeship less than a mile away at Landis Lund, a precision grinding company based in Keighley that made crankshaft grinders for Ford and the like. Since then they have been bought out and renamed Fives Landis, but I prefer the original name the company was set up under: John Lund Ltd.

Looking back, I probably shouldn't have bothered with the apprenticeship. Yes, I was Apprentice of the Year at one stage, I have all the qualifications to be a fitter and I can do pipework and all that, but it was hard work. I was there at half six in a morning, back home at four, then I'd be in the garage until midnight working on the stock cars. A few hours asleep, then I'd be back at work. I was certainly taught a few things by the guys there but most of it I have never used and I knew I never would. I spent four years on a crap wage – I started on £50 a week and ended on £90 a week – not very much to run a stock car on. And before I knew it, I had to pay for all my own racing because I was cut off from my dad. That certainly came out of the blue.

My first meeting on shale at Long Eaton (can you make out my dad's dirty car next to me?) and on tarmac at Northampton

3

My first ever F1 race in my first ever F1 meeting. I start from the back of the grid with a big black X on the back of my car. It gives me a little bit of breathing space, a chance to go slowly before the rest of the cars come charging past. At least, that's what is supposed to happen.

I line up right at the back and the first car in front of me is a superstar, number 212. My dad. He carries the silver roof of the National Points Champion, a title he has won three years in a row.

As the green flag waves, I floor the accelerator and the tyres find decent grip on the shale. That's a surprise considering that it's been bucketing it down all day, but I just grin and put the car in a straight line so I can pick up speed as quickly as possible. I look ahead and see that I'm gaining on Dad. As we near the end of the home straight, I'm getting really close to him. I start to wonder about what to do. Should I hit the National Points Champion on the first ever corner of my first ever race? Or should I try to pass him around the outside?

Suddenly Dad's car swings to the left around the corner. I turn the steering wheel to follow him, but nothing happens. My car slides straight on and bounces off the fence. I try to get back on the racing line, thankful that I'm wearing a helmet so nobody can see my red face.

It was 10 October 1987, four days after my sixteenth birthday, when I first raced a Formula 1 stock car. I never struggled with the decision to go straight into F1. It was always going to be.

I climbed out of my Ministox for the final time at Northampton the weekend before, then spent the next few days making sure my F1 was ready for its debut. I'd started building it earlier that year, ready for this moment. That first car is a bit of an icon now! It was based on the ones that my dad was racing, although I had one car for both surfaces while my dad had separate shale and tarmac cars. As if to emphasise that I was a new boy, my car was all white – white roof and white body – with blue bumpers. Compared with most cars now – in fact, compared with most cars at the time – the signwriting was pretty rudimentary. It had my name written on the side underneath the bonnet and a hopeful 'sponsor required' on top of the wing. Alongside that was a massive 515, also on both sides of the wing, underneath the cab on both sides, and on a panel behind my head. It was pretty easy for spectators to pick out my number! I'd chosen 515 because it was a mirror image of 212 upside-down. I don't know whether I ever thought that I'd change to 212 when my dad retired, but he hung around for so long that by the time he did eventually go I was 515 all the way.

That first meeting at Long Eaton involved a lot of waiting around. It started on Saturday afternoon, when the drivers involved in the Screensport series had three races to decide who won that particular championship. As it turned out, the points were tied at the end, with John Lund and my dad finishing on the same total. They had a three-lap run-off to decide the winner. John Lund got away at the start and my dad missed hitting his back bumper, after which the race was basically over.

The Screensport series probably helped me control my nerves because it gave me something to do during the afternoon. My dad was involved in all three races and the run-off and the weather meant that shale clogged up everything and needed clearing, so there was plenty to do on his car between races. By the time the evening came around and the normal meeting started, I'd already been hard at work at the stadium for hours.

After looking like an idiot at the start of my first race by driving head on into the fence, I soon managed to get going again and started to understand how to modify my driving to suit the awful conditions, although the fence gave me a flat tyre and I had to end the race on the centre. I was no stranger to driving an F1, I was used to taking my dad's car out on track occasionally and taking it for a spin around the fields on the farm, I just needed to get used to race conditions. I didn't place in any of the races, but considering that the Grand National was cancelled because they ran out of time, I didn't really get much chance.

The following day was my second meeting and it was a completely different experience. This time it was on tarmac, at Aycliffe. My dad could switch to a different car, but I was in the same one. Whereas Long Eaton had more than fifty cars there, mainly because of the Screensport competition and because the evening racing was a round in the Daily Mirror Grand Prix Series, Aycliffe only had twenty-seven, so there was a lot more room on track. And they say that there were hundreds of cars back then...

I decided to start from the front this time, especially since the first race was for whites and yellows only. I did pretty well, getting my first top-ten finish, in fifth. Sure, there were only five cars that finished, but you have to start somewhere! I did one better in my heat, finishing fourth. Only drivers called John were allowed past me – Toulson, Dowson and Lund were the only ones to do so. I even beat Ray Tyldesley. In the final I was fifth out of seven finishers, and in the Grand National only seven cars finished again – this time I was fourth.

The low numbers of finishers suggests that it was a tough meeting. It certainly was! One particular incident occurred that showed me just how brutal Formula 1 stock car racing could be. Bobby Burns must have been getting more and more annoyed as the meeting went on; he didn't finish any of the races, so maybe he was having a bad day. On the last lap of the Grand National he pulled onto the centre green, then when my dad went past Bobby accelerated off and T-boned him into the fence. Then he reversed out and hit him another two times. It was a low and dirty blow, and the only reason he was stopped from doing it again was when somebody drove one of the tractors off the centre green and hit Bobby's car with it!

I knew that F1 could be dangerous and you needed to be a tough guy to drive one, but that incident, in only my second meeting, really brought it home – especially since it was my dad who was on the receiving end. No harm was done. My dad wasn't hurt and was back racing the next weekend, as was Bobby who was fined £10 – not really a big punishment. And at least I got an extra place in the Grand National because of it!

That next weekend saw my first race win. I liked Crewe straight away. It was big, bumpy and fast; out of control fast. It was quite daunting taking a rear-wheel drive stock car on shale and flooring it to sail around the corners. The difference between a 40-horsepower Ministox and a 600-horsepower F1 was huge.

I had broken my finger during the week so I had a big bandage on it, but it wasn't too painful and didn't affect my steering. I started pretty well, coming second in my heat to another white top, Mel Morris. He had only just started racing too and we spent quite a lot of that first month racing each other. Then I got third in the final and won the Grand National, despite Mark Taylor doing his best to put me in the fence about halfway through. The fact that I had won a race despite being challenged by a more experienced driver showed that I was learning quickly, although I admit that I didn't have to cope with a last-bender, since it was my dad who finished second!

That race win kick-started a great run to the end of the season. There were no more regradings so I stayed white until the season finished and I got to start at the front and really take advantage. Over the last ten meetings I won ten races including two finals. I might have even had another final win but for Ray Tyldesley's last-bender at Coventry. My first final win came at Northampton and was, I'm told, the first time for many years that a white top had won a final. I celebrated with another first, my first roll-over in the Grand National!

The second final win came in the last meeting of the season, at Scunthorpe. It was also the meeting where the Grand National Championship was raced and I'd done so well in Grand Nationals over the last month of the season that I qualified on the inside of the fourth row, just above halfway up the grid. It was a small field of drivers, but I'm told that the spectators were impressed that I really got stuck in. I managed to get past the car that started in front of me on the inside of the third row – a certain Frankie Wainman Senior – and did my best to stop him getting back past me. I held him off for a good few laps until he finally forced his way through and I finished in third. My dad finished second and was probably a bit miffed with me – if I hadn't held him up for so long he might have won!

I finished the season in forty-second place in the grading list, not bad considering that I only raced in eleven meetings – there were eighty-nine over the whole season. I had a points-per-meeting average of exactly twenty-five – the only drivers higher were my dad, John Lund, Bert Finnikin, Nigel Whorton and Len Wolfenden. I even won the track championship at Scunthorpe since there was only one meeting there. I'd start the next season from blue. The plan was to get to red as quickly as possible and then do everything I could to stay there. But things suddenly became a whole lot harder.

I found out in November 1987, just after the end of the stock car season, that my dad was having an affair. I'd known that something wasn't right for weeks, but I never imagined that my parents' marriage was about to end. Dad simply no longer wanted to be with my mum and made the decision to move on. It was obviously a heart-breaking time for the whole family, but the peculiar situation that we had on the farm made things worse. Mum and I stayed living in the house – my sister had already moved out before they split up – and my dad moved into a static caravan in the yard. Soon Alison moved in with my dad, and eventually Brian – who would become mum's new husband – moved in with her and me in the house. It was like World War Three at times.

I sided with my mum and fell out massively with my dad. At the time, I put the blame squarely on his shoulders. I didn't speak to him for a long time, for years really. I wanted nothing to do with him, but that also meant that I didn't get any help when it came to racing. I didn't really have any money – I was still an apprentice on about £50 a week – and my mum didn't really have anything either. She was in the process of splitting everything with Dad and there was a lot of financial wrangling.

Luckily I'd earned a little bit from the race wins at the end of the season which helped buy me an engine, but it certainly wasn't a top model. Mum initially carried on coming to meetings with me and there was no way she would travel with dad, so I had to sort out my own transporter to go to meetings – my dad did offer one but I insisted I bought it from him. We had to get somebody else to drive the transporter for us since I was still under seventeen and couldn't drive it. Once Brian came along, he usually drove. It probably made it worse that everything was being played out in public, that people in the pits knew what was going on and inevitably had to choose a side.

It was awful for about three years. That's three years of my mum and dad being separated but having to live next door to each other, seeing each other every day. It might seem odd, but my mum was told by her solicitor not to move until everything was sorted out. The divorce eventually came through in 1991 after a lot of bickering and my mum moved out to the village. When she did, my dad and Alison moved into the house and I swapped with them, moving into the static caravan. They did ask if I wanted to live with them but it still didn't seem right although, by that point, enough water had flowed under the bridge and I was starting to rebuild my relationship with my dad. I could empathise a little with him. Although I'm still hurt by what he did, I can imagine that he felt pushed out. It certainly wasn't a decision that he took lightly. I'm pleased to say that, many years later, my mum and dad get on better again. I wouldn't say that they are best friends, but they no longer hate each other.

I'm sure a psychologist could sit down with me and go through exactly what happened and how it affected me, but I see life in quite a simple way. It was a rubbish time in my life, I found it very hard, but it made me a determined person. I learned that if I wanted to do something, especially when I came to stock car racing, I was going to have to do it myself.

At the start of the 1988 season, I was no longer the wonderkid driving from the front of the grid and winning loads of races. Instead I was starting right in the middle of the pack, from blue, and I had all the family problems and its effects weighing me down. But nobody else really knew that and I'm sure that everybody still expected me to keep winning. For the first time, but certainly not the last, I felt the pressure to perform and keep up my reputation.

Starting from blue was certainly a whole new ball game. Instead of getting round the first corner in first place and hanging on for as long as I could, I now started in the middle of a battle and was being knocked all over the place right from the drop of the green flag. Racing was a bit different back then. Post and rope fences meant that if you put somebody in the fence, they stayed there. You had to be very aware what was going on near your back bumper.

I got singled out because I was the new kid on the block who'd had some good results and because I was my dad's son. Being a second-generation racer with a familiar surname wasn't as common back then compared to now. I had some proper battles with the big hitters of the day: John Toulson, Bobby Burns, Chris Elwell. If anybody had a go at me, I got back at them. I wouldn't back down, never have done.

Where I did struggle was with my engines. Now that I was running everything myself, I could only work with what I could afford. Frankly, I was trying to race with a pretty shoddy engine that just didn't have the power or torque compared to what many of the other drivers had. When my only engine broke in the middle of the season, I had to beg and borrow cars to race in until I could put my engine right. Ian Higgins, Phil Whittaker, Bill Bullock and Jeff Wilkinson were among the drivers who let me use their cars for meetings while mine sat in the garage, waiting for a bit of cash before it could be fixed.

I could still pull some decent results out of the bag – my first race of the new season saw me finish in second place – but race wins became an occasional thing rather than every meeting like they had before. I first passed the chequered flag in the consolation at Scunthorpe in my third meeting, but not until six meetings later did I get another win. A decent run at the start of May saw me get three wins in three meetings, but that was it until the end of the month.

It was enough to get me a red roof, though. Making it to star grade showed that I could handle it among the sport's biggest names and I've kept that red roof – unless I've been able to paint over it with a championship roof – ever since, nearly thirty years and counting.

I switched to red paint at the start of May, meaning that I would have to start closer to the back in the British Championship at Bradford on 30 May. It was a whole new ball game, now I was bundling into the first turn alongside really good drivers like Richard Ainsworth, John Cayzer, Dan Clarke and Des Chandler. All I managed was one seventh place out of my three heats so I just scraped onto the championship grid on the outside of the fourteenth row. I was the twenty-eighth out of thirty starters. So imagine my surprise when, at the end of the race, I was stood on the podium as the third-placed driver! Only Dave Berresford and Willie Harrison finished in front, I even pipped my dad to the third step.

I also made the grid of my first World Semi-Final. Not only that, I started on the inside of the third row – a pretty decent slot, alongside Nigel Whorton – but it all came to nothing as I didn't finish the race, getting caught up with Stuart Gledhill then smacked by Dave Berresford on the second lap. I wasn't too worried, I was pretty confident that I'd get plenty of opportunities to race in a World Final. For now, I was happy to get on track as much as possible and really learn the racecraft needed to win a championship.

Not the last time I'd end up in the fence with John
Lund! This early occasion is at Birmingham in 1989.

4

There are only six laps to go and I'm sat in third place. I'm closing the gap quickly to Neil Brigg and Rob Cowley, but I know that it isn't going to be easy to pass them. Having said that, it wasn't easy to pass anybody in this race. Everybody has a red roof and knows exactly what they are doing. But I've still managed to make my way forward from the second-to-last row.

Suddenly I get a stroke of luck. Neil slows down – he must have a problem with his car. Rob is following so close that he doesn't have anywhere to go and he drives straight into the back of him and loses momentum. I slip down the inside and look in my mirror to see Rob get out from behind Neil and back on the racing line. He's too far back to do anything to me, but he should slow down John Lund and prevent him challenging me for the win.

It'll be my first proper title – the 1991 Trust Fund Champion. It's taken a while to win a title, probably longer than most people expected, but I've struggled with inferior equipment. I needed a few people to come on board and give me a bit of help, but they did so because they recognised the hard graft I put in week after week, month after month.

I may have needed a bit of good fate to win this race, but sometimes you make your own luck.

It takes time to become a top driver in F1 – nobody comes into this sport and immediately wins the major titles. The few who have taken big wins in their first seasons have usually come across from different adult formulae. Rob Speak is the obvious name that jumps to mind, Nigel Green and Mick Sworder have also been on the pace quickly after switching from F2, but they are the exceptions. Not many people win a lot after coming into F1 straight away or from Ministox.

But I continued to progress in 1989, my second full season. I had built a new car over the winter, although I still only had one car for both surfaces – it wouldn't be for a few years that I could be able to afford to run two cars. Remember, I was still only seventeen years old and I was still funding my own racing after falling out with my dad.

Even so, I managed to get to superstar for the first time when the first regrading happened at the start of May. I actually flew under the radar a little bit because all the headlines were about Gaz Bott, who had jumped straight from white top to superstar after winning eleven races from the front of the grid. John Lund and Peter Falding were the top two – they would duel it out for the silver roof all season – followed by Bott and my dad. The only other superstar was Dave Berresford in sixth place.

Getting to superstar was a major achievement, but probably more of an achievement was staying there all season. Gaz Bott couldn't hang on and dropped out after a couple of months but I kept on digging away with a few race wins every month. It was tough having to pass everybody from the very back of the grid, but I didn't feel out of place alongside Lund and Falding, Berresford and my dad, or the other drivers who wore flashing lights during the season, Nigel Whorton and Ray Tyldesley.

At Boston in May, I was taken off the track on a stretcher. It was just a precaution really, they were worried about my neck and spine after I rattled the fence pretty hard. It ended my meeting early – in fact it ended the whole meeting a bit early, because they ran out of time for the Grand National – but it didn't really hold me back, because I was back racing at Crewe six days later!

The high point of the season was racing in my first World Final. I actually had less qualifying points than the previous year so I started on the outside of the sixth row at Northampton's semi-final. I drove aggressively to work my way up, knocking Andy Webb and Murray Harrison down the order on my way to a fourth-place finish.

That meant I would start the World Final on the outside of the fifth row. For the first time, I was part of the World Final experience – the big crowd at Coventry, the extra entertainment (a wheelie truck!), the building atmosphere on the parade lap. The 1989 World Final wasn't exactly a classic. Ray Tyldesley won from pole position with a flag to flag victory, I made it as high as fifth place but Bert Finnikin got past so I finished in sixth. But it was great to be part of the spectacle. My first World Final was done; now, like the rest of my career so far, it was time to push on and improve next time.

Sometimes you just need a little help. I'd shown over the two and a bit years I'd been at it that I was a good racing driver. I was able to do well in races where I needed to cope with traffic but in races where it was all about out-and-out speed – like that World Final where there were few stoppages and it was about one driver getting away – I didn't have the engine I needed. I wanted to win every race, as simple as that. I didn't want to go out and think that I'd just take part, but in certain races that's all I could do. That changed in 1990, when a decent sponsor came on board. Mick Wright approached me and agreed to buy me a new engine in return for advertising RAP and Hoosier on my car.

Don't get me wrong, it wasn't a top of the line engine that was as good as the kind of thing that John Lund and Peter Falding were using, but it was a definite upgrade that gave me a little extra reliability and speed. And the results were almost instantaneous. In 1988, I won thirteen races. In 1989, I won nineteen races. Then, in 1990 with the new engine, I won forty-four races – and that was despite losing over a month of racing in the middle of the summer.

I was banned for six weeks after an incident at Long Eaton, but it wasn't even something that happened on track. I was ready to race, waiting in the pit lane to go out, but the officials put the gate across to stop drivers going on to the track. I wanted to get out there and race but they wouldn't let me and there was a car behind – I'm pretty certain it was Ray Tyldesley – pushing me right into the gate. I got banned, but nothing happened to Ray. And anyway, if I'd been Stuart Smith or Len Wolfenden, they'd have had the gate open in a flash!

One person who did benefit from my enforced absence was my old Ministox buddy, Rob Speak. He'd already won the British and National Points Championships in Formula 2 and fancied a pop in a Formula 1. Since I was out of action, I asked Rob if he wanted to borrow my car for a meeting. On 1 July 1990 he made his Formula 1 debut in a Wainman car at Hartlepool. Racing under number 518, he took sixth in the final, although to be honest he was a bit crap – although not as bad as I was when I borrowed his Formula 2 for a meeting! After that Rob went back to F2 for a decade or so, but nine years later he'd be back and we'd get a chance to race each other again.

The Long Eaton incident was one of a few that cropped up at this stage of my career and made me feel like there was one set of rules for me and one set for everybody else. Another time I was racing and my car got stuck in the fence. The race got stopped with yellow flags but they were going to leave my car where it was for the rest of the race. They were basically using my car as a fence post, to keep the whole thing from falling down, and if somebody else rammed into my car, tough luck. But the marshals didn't know that if my car got wrecked when somebody else hit it, I didn't have a penny to get it repaired. I wasn't happy and tried to stop the race restarting by sitting on my wing. It worked – the car was shifted to safety – but I got hauled up in front of the disciplinary committee for that too.

The six-week ban meant that I missed the British Championship but I was back in time for the World Championship races, when my new engine really showed its worth. I dropped out of the Scunthorpe semi-final after getting tangled up with Gaz Bott so I had to go to Boston for the consolation semi-final. I started on the back row in a small grid of eighteen cars. It was the kind of race that I'd have really struggled in before because eighteen cars means plenty of gaps and space and not very many opportunities to use the traffic to my advantage. Now that I had a better engine though, I managed to pass everybody apart from John Wright, who started on the third row, and I got pretty close to him on the last bend. It didn't really matter. Second place was good enough for the World Final at Odsal.

I started that race on the fifteenth row, the final car on the grid apart from the three slowest overseas drivers. Then I tangled up with Andy Webb and Mark Wareham before we had even passed the green flag so the leaders lapped me. They were on their second lap before I had even started my race! It looked like a disaster, but once I got away from Andy and Mark I realised that my car was flying. I was the fastest car on track, by far the quickest, but nobody realised because they were all watching John Lund and Bert Finnikin up front. I quietly made my way past a whole load of cars and unlapped myself by passing Lundy. Although I only finished seventh, I was well pleased with the way the race had turned out.

That little bit of input from Mick Wright was the difference. I didn't need a lot, I wasn't looking for a £10,000 engine; I just needed a few hundred quid to sort my gear out. It made a big difference meeting to meeting and helped me to win the Trust Fund race in 1991. That was also at Bradford, just like the World Final, and also had a smaller than usual grid since it was only made up of red tops (and blue-top Danny Clarke, who was allowed to race as the defending champion). Again, my new and improved engine helped me get to the front. There's no way I would have been in a position to win if I'd been racing using my old, knackered engine.

I gained another vital supporter through a stroke of bad luck at the European Championship in 1991. I went out for practice before the meeting began and my engine blew up. I thought that was it, my chance had gone, until Tim Mann offered me the use of his car. Since the European Championship was separate to the rest of the meeting and he didn't qualify for the grid, the rules allowed me to use his car and he could use it in the other races. Every cloud has a silver lining. Although I'd have preferred to use my own car, when my engine blew it pushed me together with Tim and he would become hugely important over the next year or two.

The championship grid was drawn out of a hat. Peter Falding started from the front row so it wasn't surprising that he drove away to victory. I started on the outside of the sixth row and managed to come home in third. It could have been second too – I tried to overtake Jayne Bean with a big hit towards the end and, although I got past, John Lund managed to sneak through too so I stayed in third. It was an old, crap car that I raced, so getting third was a real achievement. When I got back into the pits, Tim was raving. He said that it was the best drive he'd ever seen!

Tim wasn't much of a racer himself. He was starting from white and shared a car with Jeff Alderson so didn't make many appearances. He was having a new car built by Clive Lintern but my performance in the European made him change his mind about what he was going to do with it. Instead of racing it himself, he offered to let me race it for him. Wow, what an offer!

Clive Lintern was one of the major car builders and was very close with the Whorton family. Unfortunately, my relationship with either Lintern himself or Nigel Whorton probably wasn't the best at the time. I probably should have warned Tim what would happen next! The car wasn't finished yet and Clive heard on the grapevine that Tim had offered it to me. He asked Tim if it was true. When he was told it was, he refused to do any more work on it. Tim had to go and take it away and finish it himself, which he did with Graeme Barr. Clive wouldn't give us any help or tell us how to set it up. When we asked the odd question or two, he just said, 'do what we had to do – learn it yourself' and walked off.

Clive Lintern's behaviour actually had a long-term effect on me. I was determined never to act like that myself. How can you build somebody a car and then not help them with it? When you build somebody a car, they're not just paying for the car, they're paying for your expertise and your advice afterwards too. Once I started building cars, I made sure that I helped the drivers with them until they get it right, and even after that to keep it right.

Anyway, despite the fact that the car was thrown together at the end, we learned how to get the best out of it and within a few meetings I was beating Nigel Whorton time after time. I wanted to rub it in Lintern's face, just to piss him off. He presumably didn't like the fact that I was starting to get involved in building cars for other people, so I might take some of his business. Maybe he didn't like the fact that I kept giving him work to do, because I quite regularly put Whorton into the fence. But I just couldn't stop myself doing it! It was such fun, probably because they had loads of money and spent it like it was going out of fashion.

Tim and I learned so much from each other. He just loved to be involved. He wasn't so bothered about being in the driving seat because he didn't like the contact involved in stock car racing, but he loved to be a crew manager. Everything on tarmac was paid for by him, I just took the car on track and drove it, leaving me to look after everything on shale. It also meant that I became a two-car driver for the first time. For the first time I had a small-block tarmac special and a big-block shale shifter, something which would become increasingly common over the next few years.

The new Tim Mann car gave me a second place and two thirds in its debut meeting at Northampton. That was enough to keep me in with a shout for the Grand Prix Series at the end of the season – think the National Points Shootout but without a silver roof – where I trailed John Lund with two rounds to go, on consecutive days at Long

Eaton and Boston. Going to Long Eaton, I decided to give it a real go. To be honest, I'd already tried at Coventry the day before Northampton, where I gave John Lund a big whack. He ended up rolling and not finishing the final but I rolled over too and also didn't finish!

This time I did a better job. I waited until the last bend, when Lund went into the corner in the lead. I was in second place and Gary Lenton was taking the corner too. The end result was me taking the win and John finishing with the front of his car stuck in the fence and the back of Gary's sitting on John's roof! That propelled me to the top of the Grand Prix points chart and the only way Lundy could beat me was by stopping me from finishing in the final. I lost my rear offside tyre and had to retire, but luckily for me John had clipped another car and damaged his steering. It was a mistake very unlike him, but I wasn't complaining! I started the season by winning the Trust Fund race; I finished it as the Grand Prix Series Champion.

You need a bit of luck now and then, a leg up to keep you going. If Tim Mann hadn't got involved, I wouldn't have been competitive at the top end of the sport. Mick Wright also gave me a helping hand when it was needed. Through their help, by the end of 1991 I was the third-best driver in Formula 1 stock cars, according to the National Points Championship anyway. Only John Lund and Peter Falding were better, although the points also suggested that there was quite a gap between them and me. Time to try to narrow that a little.

British Champion 1992 – a major title at last!

5

Halfway through the British Championship race and it's go-ing pretty well so far. I didn't expect to be close to the front but it's been a hard race and plenty of those who started in front of me are already parked up on the centre green or against the fence.

Only three drivers are between me and victory. But what a three: Dave Berresford, Bobby Burns and John Lund. This isn't going to be easy.

It's going to take something special. Suddenly a chance materialises. Bobby goes a little wide and John looks down the inside, but he hasn't checked his mirrors first. I keep my foot on the accelerator and smack John as hard as I can. He drifts wide and into Bobby. I've hit Lundy hard so they both keep going wide and swipe the fence – it's not enough to put them out of the race but it's plenty to allow me to get up the inside and safely away down the straight. Two down, one to go, and it hasn't cost me much time, so I can still see Dave Berresford. I've got half a race to catch him and make a bid for my first major championship title.

I did better than close the gap to John Lund and Peter Falding in the National Points. I overtook them. My start to 1992 was pretty impressive – I won the final of the opening meeting at Northampton to become the first leader of the points table; then followed up with four wins in five races at the second meeting, at Scunthorpe. I took a heat, final and Grand National sweep at the next Northampton too, meaning that by the end of the first grading period I sat on top of the list for the first time.

True, it was only for one month – John Lund recovered from a shaky start to overtake me by the time the next grading list was published – but I hung on in second place for the rest of the year. Although John Lund ended up winning the silver roof by a comfortable margin, I had overtaken Peter Falding, despite racing in a couple fewer meetings over the year.

Fourth place in the National Points went to Paul Harrison. It was inevitable that I'd be compared with Paul during my early years. We were both the sons of well-known superstars so our first few seasons came under more scrutiny than the typical driver. Compared to nowadays, when it seems that nearly every driver is the son or relation of another driver, back then second and third generation racers were rarer.

Paul is two and a half years older than me so he had a couple of seasons more experience than me in F1 – he started at the beginning of 1986 while I jumped in at the tail end of 1987. He was a little slower to get going though, spending most of those two years as a blue top while he built up experience. He progressed to red in 1988, just like I did, and although I was the first to superstar, Paul made it the following year. So it was with a little bit of envy that I watched Paul lift the British Championship trophy in 1991 and become the first one of us to win a major championship. I trailed in sixth after starting too far down the grid to challenge in a wet race.

I didn't have any doubt that I'd win championships too, but I was starting to think that I was overdue one. I thought that my chance had gone during the 1992 British Championship at Coventry since I started on the sixth row after a pretty shoddy showing in the heats. However, the race was an attritional affair and I ground my way towards the front, getting to second by thumping John Lund into Bobby Burns. After that I just needed to close the gap to Dave Berresford. There's no doubt that it would have been hard to get the lead from him in a good clean fight, but it wasn't that kind of a race. Instead I sailed into the lead unchallenged after Dave hit Barry Heath, who had just clattered the fence. In the moment I took the lead, Bez was facing the wrong way. I had less than five laps to go to take victory and my first major championship trophy.

It felt like I'd finally arrived. For a couple of years I'd been hanging around on the outside, looking in as other drivers took the silverware. Finally, it was my turn. It felt good!

I'd turned a corner, both on the track and in my home life. I was winning big races and, after some shaky years, I was getting on better with Dad again. It probably helped that Mum had moved away from the farm so the day-to-day conflict was gone. Dad and Alison announced that they were expecting a child too, and Danny subsequently arrived at the end of 1992. I've always enjoyed being around kids, so I spent plenty of time looking after Danny as he grew up. I've lost count of the number of times people have assumed that he is my son rather than my little brother, but I guess that's bound to happen with a twenty-one year age gap!

I had also moved away to live in Preston with my girlfriend at the time, Maria. It meant I had an hour's drive to work and back each day. I was still spending lots of time working on my stock cars on the family farm so I was putting in long hours. Eventually it caught up with me. I was pretty used to crashing in my stock car, but on my way to work at Landis Lund on one July morning I fell asleep behind the wheel and collided head-on with another car. I was going uphill in a Peugeot 205 and drifted to the middle of the road. It was a very wide road and what wasn't clear was why the other driver was so close to the middle of the road too, all the witnesses said that they didn't make any attempt to avoid me. I was hardly moving, the other car was doing a decent speed, so I got sent backwards down the hill. The engine fell out and everything – it was a decent crash!

Straight away, I knew it was bad news because my leg was killing me. The front of the car caved in and my leg bent back underneath the seat. An ambulance was called and took me to the hospital. My car certainly wasn't taking me anywhere and I was convinced that I'd broken my leg. I got examined all over, they x-rayed my leg, and they also took x-rays of a lump on my arm. Then the doctor came in and told me he had good news – I hadn't broken my leg. Brilliant! But there was bad news – I had broken my arm. What? It was a clean break through my arm. I was in agony as soon as he told me but it hadn't hurt before then! There's no decent time to break a bone, but for me it was particularly bad. It was 16 July 1992, right in the middle of the stock car season.

I had about two and a half weeks until my World Championship semi-final at Hartlepool. The doctors said that there was no way I'd make it, so we thought about some contingency plans. I could race in the consolation semi but to do that I had to start at Hartlepool. Should I grid up and pull onto the centre green as soon as the race started? Would even I be allowed to do that? But what would be the point in going to the consolation semi and battling for a place in the top two if it only got me a place on the back of the World Final grid? After all, I started at the back at Bradford in 1990 and despite driving really well still only managed to finish seventh.

I decided to give it a go at Hartlepool. I tested out my arm the day before at Coventry and didn't really have any problems. In fact, better than that, I finished every race on the podium. The next day at Hartlepool I started the semi-final on the outside of the front row and led the race twice, eventually finishing second to John Lund, and I'd have beaten him if he hadn't overtaken me during yellow flags. During the rest of the meeting I won the final and came third in the Grand National from the lap handicap. Broken arm? No problem!

The couple of weeks away from racing helped me get cracking on my next project, a new shale car. The original plan had been to save it for the new year but my old car got battered at Crewe. Rather than spend hours trying to fix that, I decided to rush the new car ready to debut it at the World Final at Bradford. This one was going to be a little bit special. Tim Mann's help had given me a real boost on tarmac, now I hoped that we could do the same on the loose. There were lots of small but significant improvements: shifting the weight to the inside, offset axles, coilover shock absorbers on all four corners. However, the big boost I had was with the engine. Just like when I struggled on tarmac, what I really lacked was a decent power unit on shale. Tim Mann stepped up to the plate again, providing me with a good small-block Chevy, the first time I'd used a small block on shale.

An ideal start would have been for the new car to fly off into the distance in the World Final but that wasn't going to happen. Danny Clarke started one row ahead of me, in pole position. He skewed sideways on the green flag, leaving me stuck behind, and I got shunted into the fence on the first corner. Although I got going again, I was too far back to be in contention and ended up finishing ninth. So the new car didn't get a chance to prove itself, although results over the next couple of years would show that it was certainly an improvement over the old one, just not quite as revolutionary as I hoped.

1992 had been a decent year, the highlight of which was lifting the British Championship trophy, but the bigger achievement was stepping up to second in the National Points. The next year was a similar story with me in second place at the end of the season, although this time John Lund and Peter Falding swapped places. I actually sat in third place for most of the season but pipped Lundy at the end of the season thanks to three final wins in October. I also did pretty well in the World Final, finishing fifth after only making it onto the grid through the consolation semi-final. It would have been third had I not fluffed a move against Kev Smith with two laps to go. Instead of celebrating on the podium I crossed the line with a flat tyre.

My biggest victory in 1993 was nothing to do with stock cars, however. It was winning over the woman who would go on to become my wife.

I'd known the Dorrell family for a long time. Pete was the first to race a stock car. He mainly turned out at Northampton but occasionally at other tracks too. My dad used to help him out, giving him a hand in the pits if he needed it and helping repair his car. Then Pete's son, Shane, started racing properly in 1990 and was a regular throughout the nineties.

At a Coventry meeting in 1993, I spotted Shane's little sister, Samantha, in the pits. Although she was younger than him, she turned out to be eighteen months older than me – I was twenty-two, she was twenty-three. Sam looked pretty hot to me and we started flirting straight away. I used to throw things at her in the pits – little pebbles, bits of paper – to get her attention. What a romantic I was! But it worked because I used to get plenty of smiles. She certainly didn't tell me to bugger off and stopping chucking stuff at her!

Shane bought a car from me which brought the families a little closer together. Sam and I got a chance to have a good chat when the Dorrells travelled to the Netherlands with us. After that, we'd regularly ring each other up. These were the days before mobile phones so it needed a bit of organisation to make sure that both of us were home at the same time and you never knew who was going to answer. At meetings, we'd find excuses to leave the pits and go to get something from the boot of the car in the car park – we'd wander there together and have a kiss and a cuddle. One time, I turned up at the Dorrell house in Malvern with my lorry and mechanics after a race meeting. I announced that it was too late to drive home so we'd have to stay over and drive back the next day, but it was all an excuse to see Sam.

Soon there was no denying it, we were a couple. We always had a family gathering on the farm on 5 November and Sam was invited to that year's Wainman bonfire. She pootled up from Worcestershire in her little Fiat Uno, stayed a few nights, and basically never left!

I was lucky that I found my soulmate at a stock car meeting. Stock car racing is such a massive part of my life that I'd never be able to be with somebody who wasn't interested in the sport. But luckily, Sam is. Since we met in 1993, she must have been to over a thousand meetings. Being my girlfriend, and soon my wife, meant that everybody knew who she was. It means we can't keep any secrets – everybody knows who we are and it seems like our whole life is lived in public view. It's like a stock car version of *The Truman Show*!

Celebrating a win at Baarlo in 1998, the same year I
became the Dutch World Champion

6

It's my seventh season of racing but only the second time I've been in the World Long Track Championship at Baarlo, and the first time I feel like I've been in with a chance.

I'm on the inside of the sixth row, the third-fastest Brit in qualifying. But the ten cars in front of me contain some of the greats of long track racing: Ron Kroonder, Piet Keijzer, Chris Bimmel, John Lund and Peter Falding.

When the green flag falls, the cars roar down the long home straight and into the first corner. Bimmel bangs Keijzer from behind and both go into the fence, followed by most of the Dutch cars. I stick to the inside and exit the corner with only three car in front: Kroonder, Lund and Falding. Then Falding suddenly pirouettes onto the infield – his engine has let go and he's skidded on his own oil.

On the back straight I'm already in the podium places with only Kroonder and Lund to catch. I've been avoiding the Long Track Championship for the past few years, but in the space of one long, quick corner, everything has changed. Now I'm hooked on long track racing.

One of the things I enjoy most about our sport is the opportunity we get to travel across the English Channel to compete on a mostly level playing field with our Dutch cousins. I say mostly level because there is the odd difference in rules and set up between the two countries, but they are similar enough that Brits are competitive in the Netherlands and the Dutch are competitive in the UK.

I didn't wait long for my first taste of racing with the cloggies. At Christmas 1987, when I'd only been in F1 for a couple of months and was still a blue top, I took a trip across to race in the Christmas meeting at Baarlo. I enjoyed the experience, but racing on the long track was something else. It was a kilometre in length, about three times longer than the normal tracks I raced on in Britain, so it needed a completely different driving style and completely different car setup. On British tracks, you only keep your foot on the throttle briefly on the straights before you're getting ready to turn into the next corner. At Baarlo, it would be foot to the floor and picking up speed as you rocket down the straight.

I was keen to have a go in the World Long Track Championship, the Dutch equivalent of our World Final, but I knew that I'd have no chance of winning with my car as it was in that first full season. I'd need to alter the gearing and the brakes to suit the long track – that I could handle – but without a decent engine, I'd always be down on power. So, in 1988, I headed across the English Channel with my car and an agreement to rent an engine from Koos Peeters when I got there.

I wouldn't have made it if Peter Falding had got his way. We set off to go to the Netherlands with a new bus. Remember this was the period when I'd fallen out with my dad so was having to sort out my own transport. The coach had been altered to take the stock car but wasn't finished yet and the seats weren't even bolted in properly. We made it to Dover and parked up at a cheap hotel. I had a room in the hotel, so did my mum, but most of the lads who were mechanicing decided to sleep on the bus. The next morning, I woke up and looked out of the window. No coach!

I charged out of the hotel and, after a quick wander, spotted the coach at another hotel down the road. It turned out that the lads on the coach had drunk a skinful and fallen asleep. Peter Falding couldn't be bothered to walk back to his hotel down the road, so he crept into the coach and drove away with it to where he was staying, not knowing that some of the lads were asleep in the back – not that they were aware of anything anyway since they were out of it! Anyway, I drove the coach back up the road and back to where it should be. I was only sixteen, so I shouldn't have been driving. It was one of the stupid things we used to do at the time, Mind you, Peter was older, so what was his excuse!

To be honest, it wasn't the only time I drove the coach when I was under age. Quite often, one of the other guys would be driving but I'd take over if they wanted to go to the toilet. One time we got pulled over by the police because there was something wrong the trailer. The only problem was that I was in the driver's seat! We did a quick but subtle swap as we came to a halt that day.

Anyway, back to the World Long Track Championship in 1988. Having been reunited with the coach and made it across the Channel, we put Koos Peters' engine in the car at the pits in Baarlo. It worked pretty well and I finished the championship race in seventh (Falding the bus thief won the title for the first time) but I quickly saw that borrowing an engine wasn't going to win me the title. 1988 was the year that Chris Elwell debuted his radical small-block tarmac special, a car which was designed with the Long Track Championship in mind, and although it never reached its full potential, it showed that tarmac racing was beginning to become more specialised – nowhere more so than at Baarlo.

So I passed on the chance to race at Baarlo in the World Long Track for the next few years. That didn't stop me racing in the Netherlands completely, though. The following year, in October 1989, I became one of the first group of Brits (with my dad, Scott McKenzie, Richard Dobson, Andy Webb and Eric Gravelling) to race in the Dutch Open Championship at Lelystad. That was a more typical quarter-mile tarmac track so I didn't have to go scrabbling around for a decent engine.

I came fifth in the first year we raced in the Dutch Open – my dad was third – then the following year I won the title. It was my biggest success at that point in my career. I had to try and avoid the Dutch drivers who were trying to take me out because they didn't want a Brit to win the title! Two years later, they were trying it again, and failing again!

I didn't try to defend the Dutch Open title in 1993 because my eyes were on a different prize. By now, I felt ready for another crack at the World Long Track Championship. I had the backing of Tim Mann which meant that I had the kind of engine that would allow me to be competitive. I'd actually intended to race at Baarlo in 1991, as soon as Tim came on board, but we'd only just started working together and there were some teething problems on the car during a practice session in the UK, so we scratched the trip. It wasn't until two years later that we got to Baarlo in my Tim Mann-sponsored tarmac car.

Ironically, I'd waited for five years until I had a good engine to compete in the Long Track Championship but it was the engine that cut short my race. We discovered an oil leak in the pre-meeting practice and thought we had it fixed, but fluctuating oil pressure meant that I had to retire after seven laps of the big race. Even so, I managed to move up to third place from the inside of the sixth row on the first lap before the race was restarted from scratch – a bad decision, in my opinion, but the oil pressure problem meant that I wouldn't have finished anyway.

Nevertheless, I fell in love with the big Baarlo track at the second time of asking. It was a different sort of racing. Being such a large track meant that racing styles were quite different. Dutch drivers have always been a bit more timid than British drivers when it comes to putting the bumper in. That was especially the case at Baarlo, where the long straights meant that making a good, clean hit was very difficult to do. I wasn't afraid to put the bumper in – being aggressive was part of the reason I won the Dutch Open twice at Lelystad – but I was much more respectful of the big oval at Baarlo and enjoyed racing in a different way. Not all the Brits were the same. Stuart Smith famously smacked Friedhelm Welters on the first lap at Baarlo in 1984, but he knew that was the only way he would have a chance of winning.

After getting bitten by the long track bug in 1993, the path to winning the championship was one of slow steps forward, year by year, although I almost ran out of time. In 1994 I was still underpowered and, despite starting as the top British qualifier, I dropped back to finish the championship race in sixth.

The next year, 1995, I was similarly off the pace, although not by as much. This time I even managed to get into the lead by the end of the first lap, overtaking Ron Kroonder with a nifty knock wide, but the race was red flagged. Just like two years before, Piet Keijzer was the reason why my great start was all for nothing. When the race started a second time, I couldn't get close enough to Kroonder and, by the time the first lap was over, I knew I wouldn't be able to catch him. It was that simple. If Kroonder got away early, there was no stopping him. I eventually finished third.

I did make one particular discovery during that particular long track campaign though, something which is still with me today. Before we set off to Baarlo, I was contacted by one of Ian Higgins' mechanics, Norm, who asked for a lift over. Norm wanted to watch the racing but Ian wasn't going that year, so I said he'd be welcome to travel with us. He came up the night before so we could set off nice and early, and Norm threw himself into the last-minute preparations going on in the garage. He looked at the car and said to me that the fuel tank didn't look big enough to cope with Baarlo. I didn't know Norm that well, so I wasn't sure whether to take what he said seriously. Eventually he convinced me to swap the fuel tank from the shale car into the tarmac car that was going to Baarlo. We both had our heads in the back of the car and were welding some brackets to hold the fuel tank in place when the fumes in the fuel tank ignited. It blew back and got the pair of us, knocking us onto our backsides. We just looked at each other and shrugged.

It was an explosive start to a long friendship. Norm has been with us ever since and is now my main setup man. I can rely on him to sort out my car and get it ready for track, which gives me the time to concentrate on customer cars – after all, they pay the bills. But despite the trust I have in Norm, it was only a few years later, when I was booking us onto a ferry to cross the Channel, did I discover that he isn't actually called Norman! That nickname comes from his resemblance to Stormin' Norman Schwarzkopf, the Gulf War general. His real name is Richard Brighton, although I suspect hardly anybody knows that.

Norm stayed around for all of my big successes, although they took a few years to come. Ron Kroonder got away again in 1996 for his fourth Long Track title in a row while I was left on the infield with a flat tyre. By now I was mimicking the Dutch drivers and designing my tarmac cars with the Long Track Championship firmly in mind, but Kroonder was definitely the one to beat.

That finally happened in 1997. I was helped by Piet Keijzer, who also knew that to win the Long Track title, he'd have to stop Ron. He rifled Kroonder into the wall on the first lap and damaged his handling. Although Kroonder was able to restart after a red flag because another car was on fire, he was definitely damaged. Instead it was a three-car race between me, Keijzer and Louw Wobbes.

With seven laps to go, Keijzer was running in the lead from Wobbes and me. When Louw went for the lead and they both went wide, I briefly put my nose in front before Keijzer carried his speed down the back straight and into the lead. Two laps later, Keijzer braked at the wrong point and I hesitated a fraction too long. Wobbes hit me into Keijzer, both Piet and I went wide, and Louw took the lead. Although I got past Keijzer too, I wasn't able to make up the gap to Wobbes because one of my rear tyres was going off.

So I finally beat Ron Kroonder, only for Louw Wobbes to nip in and take the victory. Still, second place was my best result so far, and I followed up by winning the Jac Claes Trophy and getting two more second-place finishes in the rest of the meeting.

Going into the 1998 World Long Track Championship, we all knew that it would be the last because developers had their eye on Baarlo. I was going to miss the place. Not only had I been in the last five World Long Track races, I also did four meetings at Baarlo during the season in the lead up to the championship. Each time I had to swap the big-block engine out of my shale car and put it in the tarmac car so I had the power for the long Baarlo track, then I had to switch them back once we returned. It was a lot of effort, but I knew it was going to be the last time the race was held at Baarlo. In a fairly short space of time it had turned into an iconic race for the Brits. I was certainly captivated by it and really keen to be the final champion.

All the planning nearly came to nought when the big-block engine blew up in the last Baarlo meeting before the Long Track Championship. For a while it looked like I would be screwed, but a lot of hours in the garage and a lot of money spent meant that the engine was fixed in time. Ron Kroonder actually offered me an engine if I couldn't get mine sorted in time. I was really impressed with that gesture. Ron was the man to beat, he was also really keen to be the last champion and to overtake Rien Rutjens as the driver with most Long Track titles; but he still went out of his way to offer help to one of his main opponents.

Even though the engine was fixed, I still nearly didn't make it. On the drive down to Dover, just as we were close to the ferry terminal, the gearbox went on the bus. I managed to get onto the ferry with one gear and limped to the hotel with hardly any gear changes but the gearbox went completely as I was parking up. I didn't know how we were going to get to the track or get home afterwards. Then Norm came up with a bright idea. He knew that Ian Higgins had wanted to come over to watch, but chose not to because his wife's passport had run out of date and they hadn't realised until a day or two before. I rang Ian up and told him that I was in a bit of a pickle. I could get a gearbox from Bob Handley in Leicester, but we were stuck in the Netherlands.

'Leave it with me,' Ian said. I didn't find out until later that he borrowed a van from a friend, telling him that he had a little errand to run. He drove from York to Leicester, picked up the gearbox, then legged it down to Dover for the overnight ferry. When that docked he drove to the hotel and I discovered him the next morning, parked next to our bus, asleep in the front seat of the van. My dad towed the bus to Baarlo and we spent most of the time in the pits underneath the bus, installing the new gearbox. My stock car was almost forgotten as we concentrated on being able to get home again.

When it was time for the Long Track Championship, I crawled out from under the bus to get in the driver's seat of the car. I started on the inside of the third row as the top Brit, a place I'd made my own over the past few years. When the green flag fell I managed to get around Louw Wobbes, who'd missed a gear, and came out of the first corner in second place behind Ron Kroonder. I was happy with that, but them the race was red flagged. The driver in trouble who cut short my really good start? You guessed it, Piet Keijzer again!

Wobbes got it right on the restart and didn't miss a gear, so he exited the first corner in second behind Kroonder. I was third. In past years I'd have already missed my chance and Kroonder would have driven off into the sunset, but I'd gradually narrowed the gap. The three of us broke free and, for ten long laps, I inched closer to the two cars ahead of me. Then I was close enough to make a move. I overtook Wobbes on the inside – no contact required – then set my sights on Kroonder. Three laps later, I tried the same again. I turned tighter than Kroonder at the end of the home straight and we went down the back straight side by side. And something great happened. My car gradually inched ahead. No longer was Kroonder the man to beat. This time it was me.

Eight laps were left, during which I opened up a slight gap. We're talking very fine degrees here, our speed was almost identical, but my car was just a tiny bit quicker – just like Ron had been for the previous few years. I rounded the long oval and took in the moment. This win had been six years in the making.

There wasn't much time for celebration. Straight after the race, Ian Higgins drove back to York to drop off the van with his friend. Quite what that friend thought when he looked at the milometer after Ian's 'little errand' I don't know! I did the parade lap, came back to the pits and returned to my place underneath the bus to carry on fixing the gearbox.

A lot had been thrown at me in the build up to that meeting, but it was all worth it. As far as NACO was concerned, I was the World Champion. As for the BriSCA version of the World Championship? Don't get me started on that.

1994 World Final – I think my body language says it all

7

It feels like I'm driving a rocket.

I know I'm driving the fastest car on the track. Everybody else is quick too — this is the World Final after all — but my car is so quick that I've just stormed into the lead. Paul Harrison couldn't hold me off for more than a lap, neither could Andy Smith.

There's a little bit of steam escaping from the engine. That worries me a little, but all I can do is keep the car on track, keep working the traffic and keep Andy Smith as distant as possible.

Nine, eight, seven laps to go. The gap between us increases — steam or not, my car is way quicker than Smith's. He's not even in the right vehicle; he's using his new tarmac car, one that has barely raced before.

Seven, six, five laps to go. I'm miles ahead. The steam has started to ease. Perhaps whatever the problem was has sorted itself out. Anyway, I'm starting to think about how many turns are left to the chequered flag, which is always a good sign.

Four laps to go, still on course. Andy Smith still way back. But something doesn't feel right.

Three laps to go. Everything changes. The car fills with white smoke and I have nothing under my right foot. I don't believe it. The engine has seized up, I have no power. I move to the outside of the track and try to think if there is anything I can do. Nothing. I manage to get onto the inside line and, as I park up on the inside of the corner, Andy Smith charges past.

At the start of 1994, if you had given me a choice of winning either gold or silver roof, I'd probably have picked gold. After all, it's the one we all want to win, isn't it? It's the biggest race on the biggest night of the year.

My progress to the 1994 World Final was relatively untroubled. I started a semi-final at a sludgy Stoke from pole and, although I dropped to third by the chequered flag, I wasn't too worried. The priority in the World Final is to start near the front. As long as you're on the first four or five rows, you have a chance. If you're at the back you're out of it – I'd started two World Finals from the consolation berths and, despite having the drives of my life, still finished off the podium.

The last time there had been a World Final at Bradford, two years before, I debuted a new shale car. I had a new shale car for this one too, but I gave myself plenty of time to bed it in before the big race. A new car always requires slight changes to the handling and how it runs because the minor adjustments and differences introduced during the building process all have knock-on effects. The new car rolled out on track for the first time at King's Lynn in June – probably a good job since I didn't quite have the set up right and the car had a tendency to spin. It actually happened mid-race in the semi-final, leaving me sat across the racing line, but luckily I was clear of any traffic so could right myself and get going before I was hit in the side.

I started the World Final on the inside of row three – for some reason the top-seeded foreign drivers started on the fourth row that year – and dropped back a place at the start, but I wasn't too worried because I set up the car for the dry at the end. I soon realised that I was lightning quick. I had the quickest car on track by far. I got back past Rob Cowley within a lap or so then sneaked up the inside when Kev Smith went after Dave Berresford. After four laps I was third and the only guys in front were with Paul Harrison and Andy Smith, the new kid on the block. A few laps more and I nudged Paul aside for second. After ten laps it was Andy's turn and I was leading the World Final.

Little did I know that on one of the early laps a fan blade sheared off and it went straight through the bottom hose. I didn't know anything about it at the time, but the water slowly began to leak out. When you lose water in an engine, you don't see it and you don't feel it until something starts to happen.

Almost as soon as I took the lead, I noticed steam starting to creep out from underneath the bonnet. The temperature gauge started to go up a little but it still read okay and didn't go too high. I didn't know what the problem was or how serious it might be. I still had full power and easily whipped past a few backmarkers. Andy Smith had dropped way back and I was miles ahead with five to go. Even better, the steam was beginning to go away. I began to think that I had the race won. The trouble was that the steam had stopped because there was no water left in the engine.

It all fell apart with three laps to go. With no water to cool things, the pistons had melted through. Coaxing the car through the final laps wasn't an option – there was zero power. All I could do was glide round a lap or so as the car gradually lost speed, then park up just as Andy rocketed past. He coolly wound down the final couple of laps to the chequered flag. It was his first World Final and he won it through pure luck.

It devastated me. It broke me. It smashed me to bits. Had I been second or third, it wouldn't have mattered so much, but I had been leading the World Final with three laps to go. Why would something like that happen? We all go through disappointments in life, but that was bad. The crew and my family were all devastated, the sponsors were too.

What made it worse was that it wasn't anybody's fault, I couldn't blame anybody. It was just fatigue on the metal fan, something that could go at any time. I tried to blame myself. I tried to persuade myself that I should have seen it before the race. But I was just looking for a reason when there wasn't any. I might have picked it up if I had looked at the fan blades, but there are thousands of parts in an engine. What do you check, what don't you check? If it was a hairline crack, would I have even seen it? You could replace the entire engine just in case something like that happens. There wasn't any point in getting down on myself.

If I had been put in the fence, well that's racing, that's different. If that had happened, a stock car driver would have beaten me in a stock car race and, although it might have been tough to take, ultimately I'd have been beaten by a better driver on the day. But instead it was just one of those things.

I was gutted. Andy was ecstatic. As he parked up and stood on his wing to wave the chequered flag at the crowd, I just stood there, struck dumb, with my hands on my hips. He knew he hadn't won, really. I had got past him and left him for dust. It must have been a weird feeling for him to have won his first World Final like that, but I guess that's what happens. I've won my share of races through good luck too, just not in World Finals! But everybody was talking about him and his dad being the first father and son World Champions. That should have been me and my dad.

That night, Saturday 24 September 1994, was the night that I lost interest in the gold roof. I vowed that I would win the silver that year instead. That was the only thing I was going to do. I had led the points chart for most of the season, but it was always a close thing. At the first regrading I was only three points ahead of Peter Falding, by the time the World Final came around there were still less than 100 points between me, Peter and John Lund. But there was no doubt in my mind that the National

Points title was going to me after the World Final disappointment.

It didn't stop me wanting to win every race, not at all. Every race I've entered I've wanted to win, some might say too much, but making a conscious decision to go for the silver roof made me consistent. It made me make sure I travelled to every meeting possible. That's something I've carried for more than twenty years since and it's still the same now, it's what I do. Would I rather stop at home? Not at all.

There were twelve meetings left after the World Final. I attended them all, as did Falding and Lund. Both Peter and I improved slightly over the last month or two, bumping up our points-per-meeting average slightly, with us both finishing on an average of 27. The actual gap between us was 48 – 1672 to 1624 – and over the course of the season I raced in 62 meetings to his 60. Yes, that means if he had turned up at two more meetings and scored at the same rate he did over the rest of the season, he'd have beaten me by six points. But he didn't. To win the National Points Championship you need to score consistently high scores over as many meetings as possible. If he didn't turn up, that's not my problem. The silver roof went to the driver who wanted it more.

I set my stall out. This was what I was going to do. The silver roof was where it was at. Whatever happened with the gold roof, well, whatever. It was just one race, anybody could get lucky, just like anybody can get unlucky.

At the end of 1994, if you had given me a choice of winning either gold or silver roof, my answer wouldn't have been the same as at the start of the season. I wouldn't have picked gold. And I'd probably have thrown in a few swear words too!

Ready to do battle in New Zealand in 1997 with my
Rotorua-based car – Stan Hickey looks on from the
driver's seat

8

When you're in the lead in a stock car race, you know you've got a target on your back. But this is something else.

It's the third and final race of the World 240 Championship at Palmerston North in New Zealand. I came into this race leading the points but there's no way that the Kiwi drivers are going to sit back and let a foreigner win their premier title.

I've tried to keep them unaware that I don't have any power steering and my car is harder to control, but eventually they catch up with me. Craig Boote has been after me since the green flag dropped, so have plenty of others. I get taken into the wall and a brake pipe shears. Great. Now I have no power steering and no brakes.

But I still have a working engine and four wheels, so I reverse out of the wall and get back going again. If they're going to stop me, they'll have to do better than that!

In November 1994, only about eighteen months after we met, Sam and I got married. I'm sure plenty of people thought it was a shotgun wedding because Sam was pregnant, but that wasn't the case. It just felt right, we were in love. Sam had already been living in Silsden for almost a year and everything had worked out, so why not go ahead and get married?

Since we already had a place to live on the farm, we didn't need many things like kitchen equipment and new towels. So when people asked us what we wanted as a wedding gift, we asked them to contribute to our honeymoon in New Zealand. Sam's parents and brothers had already visited there and loved it but neither of us had been, so we settled on a trip of a lifetime down under. We expected it to be a one-off trip – little did we know that we'd end up going back almost every year since then!

That trip in January 1995 coincided with the New Zealand superstock season but I wasn't out there to race. Sam and I went to the track at Palmerston North expecting to watch five other Brits – John Lund, Peter Falding, Andy Smith, Paul Harrison and Chris Elwell – compete for the World 240 Championship. We were wandering around the pits when Graham Elwell, Chris's dad, came up to us. He asked if I had my racing gear with me. I did, it was in the motorhome, I'd brought it with me in case I got a chance to try driving a superstock at the end of a meeting or something. 'Go and get it,' Graham told me. 'Chris has vertigo and can't race. Get in his car!'

With hardly any preparation, I found myself on track in New Zealand's premier championship, in a car I'd never raced before, in a formula I'd never raced before. I had a chance to test the car in a couple of practices during the afternoon, but that was it.

That year, the championship was run over two nights. The first had two heats, the second evening had a third heat. The positions in those three races decided the grid for the championship race. I started the first heat from the inside of the eleventh row with Andy Smith next to me and came home in eleventh place. In the second heat, Andy and I moved forward to the fourth row and I guided the car home for another finish. That put me in fifth place in the standings after two heats, the top Brit. Paul Harrison and Peter Falding made the top ten, but Andy Smith and John Lund were already as good as out of the running.

That night in the bar, Graham Elwell overhead the other Brits saying that they were going to take me out the next evening. Graham went mental. I didn't really know the Elwells too well but I knew that Graham could be a bit of a scary dude at times. That conversation did not impress him at all. To win the 240 Championship, a driver needs the support of his teammates. Usually, the best-placed driver from a particular track is helped by the other drivers from the same place – they'll try to guide him to the front or try to take out his opponents by crashing into them. It's a form of racing that's particular to New Zealand and reflects the fact that drivers tend to be registered with a specific track, but the British drivers had no intention of doing the same to help me. They were going to do the exact opposite. They'd rather a Kiwi won the title than me.

Even without their help, I still finished the third heat in sixteenth and retained my position as the top overseas driver, although I'd dropped to eighth overall, so I started the championship race on the outside of the fourth row with Peter Falding on the inside of the fifth. But it didn't take long for the Kiwis to find me. I overtook Dave Evans, a local with a reputation for taking out the opposition, and although I managed to puncture his tyre on my way past, he still rode me up the wall so I rolled over and landed back on my wheels in the middle of the track. Race over. Without the help of my fellow countrymen, I had no chance of joining Chris Elwell as a foreign winner of the World 240 title.

But I would get another chance to race in the championship again. The opportunity stemmed from a chance conversation during my honeymoon. When Sam and I arrived in New Zealand, Lyall Rumney from Rotorua had just won the New Zealand Championship. I found Lyall in the bar one night with two of his sponsors, husband and wife Stan and Sonja Hickey. As reigning New Zealand Champion, Lyall had the opportunity to race in the Formula 1 World Final, so I offered to provide him a car for his time in the UK. The Kiwi drivers who came across were usually given any spare car that was available, which usually meant they had to race a piece of crap, but I told them that I'd provide a decent machine. It wasn't easy. Lyall arrived in the UK in September 1995 after Tim Mann had moved on but before my new sponsor Tony Cole got involved, so I was short of financial backing. But I knew I could find a car and Lyall ended up racing in Shane Dorrell's machine. It was a good car, originally built by Clive Lintern.

I refurbished the car and got it all painted up for him, and it was certainly a good performer. Lyall raced in the Hednesford World Final that Keith Chambers won and, despite starting from the back row, he ended up in fourth place – still the best result by a Kiwi in the World Final.

Stan and Sonja said that they would return the favour for me and I could use Lyall's car the next time I was over. I didn't make the trip the following winter but said that I was keen to race there in the winter of 1996-97. A few months into the next season, Sonja rang me up – I think she'd had a few glasses of wine – and told me that they had bought a car for me to use in New Zealand. Lyall understandably didn't want to stop racing for the few weekends I'd be over, so Stan and Sonja had gone and bought me a superstock!

Sonja rang me up again a few weeks later – a little drunk again – and said to me, 'Would it be okay if Stan raced the car in the New Zealand Championship?' I said, 'Sonja, it's your car, why are you even asking me?' But she insisted it was mine, that they had bought it for me to race. Anyway, Stan jumped in it a couple of times before I got to New Zealand and gave the car a bit of a shakedown. It must have helped, because the first time I drove it, it was great straight away. In total, I was in New Zealand for about six weeks. The first time I raced was on New Year's Day in the Grand Prix meeting at Palmerston

North. Sonja came up to me in the pits and gave me the names of three drivers: Craig Boote, Barry Hunter, and the guy who had taken me out two years before, Dave Evans. 'They are the three hardest drivers,' she told me. 'Don't mess them about.'

I went out in the first race and fenced all three of them. Back in the pits, Sonja came up to me and said, 'Did you hear what I said?' 'Yeah,' I replied. 'Oh. Okay.' I left her stuck for words. I had decided to stake my claim. John Lund came up to me and told me that it was a bad idea, that I'd never win anything in New Zealand by racing like that. Actually, I thought I might.

Racing in New Zealand for an extended period gave me a chance to take in some of the island. On one occasion we were driving around the South Island and we pulled up at the side of the road to look at the seals playing the sea. A car pulled up behind us and a couple got out. They saw the race-car transporter and asked us where we were racing. It turned out that they were from on holiday from Hartlepool and they said that they would try and make it to the next meeting – which, as it turned out was the World 240 Championship at Palmerston North.

If the first time I raced the World 240 Championship was a bit of a shambles, this time it was anything but. Among the other Brits racing were my brothers-in-law, Shane and Clinton Dorrell. John Lund was there and had come round to the thinking that if a British driver was going to win, he'd need the support of his countrymen. Gaz Bott and Russell Taylor also made the trip. Through Lyall Rumney and the Hickeys, I'd also forged a good relationship with the drivers at Rotorua. When it came to the crunch, that helped me too.

This time the championship was the usual World 240 format with points gathered over three heats used to decide the winner – there was no championship race. I managed to score well in the first two heats and went into the final race leading the points, but I wasn't unscathed. One of the impacts in the second heat had damaged the power steering. Stan and Sonja were all for loading the car up because they said it wasn't driveable without power steering – all Kiwi cars had it at that stage. But I wasn't having that, there was no way I wasn't going to give it a go. I told them that I'd drive anything.

We messed about with the power steering for as long as we could before the final race but the pump was wrecked, we couldn't do anything with it. It was a case of give up or race with no power steering. Then, as I was climbing in the car to get belted in, I had a brainwave: get rid of the power steering oil. With the oil gone it's just a box, a mechanical box, so at least I wouldn't be forcing the oil round by hand. I jumped out of the car and pulled all the pipes out, dumping the oil. It was a close-run thing, I nearly missed the gate closing, but I made it with seconds to spare.

To be honest, it wasn't that bad. The car wasn't perfect, but it was driveable. Now I needed to stay out of danger. Although I got taken into the wall and lost my brakes, I just kept going and going. I drove into everything, round everything and through everything. It just all came together perfectly. Despite all the problems, it was one of those occasions where it wasn't going to go wrong. I crossed the finish line down the places but with enough points to take the World 240 title.

To win in New Zealand, you need to be prepared to put the bumper in. After I won the World 240 trophy, I had drivers come up to me saying that they watched the first time I raced that year at Palmerston North, when I took out the Kiwi big guns, and decided that they wouldn't mess with me. If I showed I could go in as hard as anybody else then I wouldn't get picked on. They're only cars, it's only metal. I'd been in the fence a lot of times too, so I wasn't worried about that side of it!

Later on in the evening after I'd won the World 240, the same chap who had pulled over at the side of the road when we were watching the seals came and found me in the pits. He told me that my win had made his holiday and handed over an envelope, telling me to buy all the guys who had helped a drink. I pocketed it, thinking nothing of it, and carried on packing away. Later on I opened up the envelope and found £200 inside. £200! That was a lot of money to me back then, it was enough to buy all the guys a bottle of champagne, never mind a drink. When I found him again he wouldn't take it back. I eventually got it changed into New Zealand dollars and we celebrated that night. Boy, it was messy.

I later found out that the same couple gave John Lund £5,000 for winning the World Final, effectively doubling his prize money. Then, last year, I was approached by a chap who runs Silksworth Aquatics in County Durham, offering me a bit of sponsorship. When I got talking to him, he told me that his parents used to watch stock car racing and had helped out a few drivers in the past. I worked out that he was the son of the couple who gave me that welcome little bonus in New Zealand! It's funny how these things come around sometimes.

Anyway, it wasn't a surprise to find out that the Kiwi drivers weren't keen on me winning their main title again. I still ended up with fifth place in the World 240s in 1999, although I wasn't travelling to the other side of the world for fifth. It didn't help that John Lund and I were the only Brits racing so neither of us had the support that we needed to have a crack at the title. Although John did exactly what he wanted to when he rifled Stan Hickey into the wall. John blamed Stan for taking him out of the previous year's World Final at Coventry – more on that later – and he travelled to the other side of the world for a chance to get him back. They do say that revenge is a dish best served cold!

Remembering what it was that won me the World 240 three years before, I arrived in New Zealand in 2000 determined to put the boot in early. And I did just that. Craig Boote was the top dog in Kiwi racing at the time, having won the domestic New Zealand Championship three times in four years. I arrived in New Zealand in time to take part in the Grand Prix meeting at Nelson and made sure I put Boote into the fence hard, breaking one of his shock absorbers and taking him out of the running. I was sending another signal to the Kiwi drivers – I was here to compete again. I finished second in the Grand Prix to Tony McLanachan but hoped to go one better in the World 240. This time Murray Harrison and Jason Holden were there to fly the Union Jack alongside me and John

Lund (who was more in the mood to race this time!) so I'd have a bit of back up on the track.

For the first race of the 240 Championship I drew grid twenty-three, starting on the inside of the twelfth row. If there was a single corner that won me the title in 2000, it was the first corner of the first lap of the first race. After one turn I'd moved up about ten places into the middle of the pack. In a twelve-lap race you can't hang around. I carried on the charge, including passing two cars on the last lap, to finish in second. I was well happy with that result from my worst grid position of the evening.

In the second race, I started in the middle of the grid on the outside of the fifth row. I made up some places again and also disposed of Craig Boote for a second time in a few days with a hit that knocked my own car off its wheels for a moment. Just in case anybody wasn't aware that I was in a mood to win, I was making it crystal clear! I finished that race in third.

Two podiums were always going to give me a great chance and going into the last race I was top of the standings. Two points behind was Kelvin Gray, a Palmerston North driver who had won the first race and finished sixth in the second, so the Palmy drivers were always going to be gunning for me in the final race.

Consistency is the key in the World 240 – make sure you finish all your races. Like three years before, I knew that I had to finish to have a chance of taking the title. I started the final race on the third row, but Craig Boote was the driver starting directly in front of me. Oops – maybe I should have thought of that before binning him! When the green flag fell, Boote stamped on the wrong pedal and would not be moved. Behind me, Wayne Hemi (another driver I'd fenced in the Grand Prix at Nelson) parked up on my back bumper, trapping me between the two.

Thankfully, one of the other Brits came to my aid. Jason Holden spotted what was going on and hit Boote, spinning him out of the way and giving me a chance to race. I had plenty to do though – my front of the grid start ended up with me taking the first corner with the tail end of the field. I stayed out of trouble after that and managed to pick my way through the traffic as the laps progressed. Boote made another attempt to stop me on the last lap but he fluffed it and I drove around the outside to finish in fifth. One place ahead of me was Kelvin Gray – he had only managed to close the gap by one point, so I just stayed on top – the final standings were Frankie Wainman Junior on 71, Kelvin Gray on 70. I'd won my second World 240 title, only the second driver to win it more than once. I was ecstatic. I'd taken on the Kiwis on their home turf, disposing of their top driver on more than one occasion.

Although I was the reigning champion, in 2001 I was so busy in the workshop that I just couldn't spare the time to defend my title. It was a really hard decision to make but I had cars in the order book for Keith Chambers, Warwick Ellis, Paul Higgins and Steve Thomas, plus my own new cars to sort out. But when I did make the long journey to the other side of the world, I was there to win. I went close to making it three titles to my name in 2003 and 2005 – both times I was third. I also came second in the North Island Championship in 2005 with my old mate Stan Hickey getting the win.

From my first trip in 1995, I fell in love with it down there – the place, the racing, the people. The racing might be confrontational on the track, but away from it there's a really great community of drivers, mechanics and fans. Oval racing is a big sport there, relative to the size of the country. Everybody knows about superstock racing in New Zealand. A couple of years ago somebody even went into a souvenir shop at the bottom of South Island and said that they had spotted Frankie Wainman Junior stickers for sale in there!

Suffice to say, the honeymoon was not the trip of a lifetime – it was the first of many trips of a lifetime.

Leading off the 1995 World Final with John Lund

9

Racing is what I do. I love it. Sometimes it makes me tense. Sometimes it makes me happy. Sometimes I'm devastated by the result. Sometimes I'm ecstatic. And sometimes I'm just bored.

Yes, bored.

I started from pole position in the World Semi-Final. I led into the first corner. I led out of it. And I've been leading ever since.

There have been a few incidents, including the need for a restart, but at no point have I ever been threatened. Andy Smith is behind me but never close enough to challenge, he seems quite happy to follow me around for second. I count down the laps – fifteen to go, ten to go, five, four, three. It was at this stage that it all went wrong in last year's World Final, but Andy isn't going to get lucky today. Two laps to go, last lap. I pass the chequered flag to take possibly the easiest win of my career.

A boring race? Yes. But have I done what I came to do? Yes.

If I had any doubt about where my priorities lay after the anguish of the 1994 World Final, 1995 proved it. I qualified from the semi-final at Hartlepool easily then started the World Final at Hednesford from the outside of the front row after John Lund won the coin toss to decide pole position. I took the lead into the first corner and led the race for five laps until Lundy battered me into the fence and I retired to the infield. Everything built up to the biggest race of the season and I managed five laps.

As it turned out, Lund only managed two laps in the lead before he was put out in almost exactly the same place by Andy Smith. He also led for two laps before Keith Chambers shoved him into some spun cars, and Keith went on to take the win.

The five laps I managed confirmed to me that the World Final wasn't about being the best – it was just about winning one race on one night. The only way to be the best driver was through the National Points Championship and the 1995 campaign was a cracker. Paul Harrison led for the first half of the season but lost first place at the September regrading. He dropped like a stone after that, not helped by missing a month of racing straight after the World Final. That was probably the closest he ever got to the silver roof – I wonder if he regrets those missed meetings now?

When Paul lost the lead, he was actually overtaken by three drivers: me, John Lund and Andy Smith. We'd fight it out over the rest of the season in what was probably the best finish to a Points Championship ever. If you wanted to know who the top drivers in the sport were in that particular year, there's your answer – it was the three of us who were slogging it out, week after week, taking it down to the last meeting.

I had started the year building a new tarmac car. It was a rush job, taking just two weeks to build, mainly because the cosy situation I'd had for the last couple of years with Tim Mann suddenly changed. Tim contacted me to say that he was going to shift his attention from Formula 1 to Eurocars; he was going to fund a car for Peter Falding to drive in that series. He was selling the tarmac stock car that I currently drove so I had to find a replacement – quickly! To be fair to Tim, he did leave me the small-block engine, but I still needed to put together a car for it to go in.

I think that Tim had got a bit tired of Formula 1 and the politics that can come with it. He had started promoting at Stoke but struggled to make ends meet there and the constant niggling over rule changes were annoying him. Some were designed to limit costs but he felt that some were being imposed just for the sake of it.

Anyway, given the short timeframe, the car that I put together was an absolute belter. New rules were coming in about weighting, only allowing 52% of the weight on the inside, so balancing the car was becoming more and more of a science. I built a slightly longer than normal chassis which allowed me to put the engine slightly further forward and in turn the seat moved forward too. Not being over the rear axle and prop shaft meant that the seat could be a little lower, which in turn lowered the height of the roll cage. It meant that the car could be six inches closer to the ground than before and shifted the weight distribution ever so slightly.

The changes worked. I won heat and final at the car's first meeting, at Northampton, following up with a third in the Grand National. A pretty decent start. I then took final wins at Hartlepool, Buxton, Birmingham and Northampton again over the first two months of the season. The only reason that Paul Harrison led the points table was that my shale form was pretty ropey in comparison, while he was more consistent over both surfaces.

I took the new tarmac car to Northampton again in May for the European Championship. The grid was pulled out of a hat and I started on the outside of the tenth row while Andy Smith and Paul Harrison were both three rows in front and Peter Falding one in front of them, so I had plenty to do. But since I was very happy with my tarmac car, I didn't mind that there were two restarts due to early crashes – the resulting retirements meant that there were gaps on the track and I could build up some speed. I gradually reeled in and passed both Falding and Smith in one corner to take the lead with five laps to go. It was my first European Championship win.

The Euro win and my performances on tarmac throughout the season showed that I was the one to beat in the World Final at Hednesford. That's why Lundy put me in the fence as soon as he could, but he couldn't do that every single weekend, so I was right up there in the points table. There was a bit of bad feeling between us after the World Final, which added to the spectacle too. John said something to me after the World Final, inferring that he was going to win the silver roof. That wound me up. I think my response was, 'If I don't win the points, I'll make sure you don't too.' I don't think he appreciated that!

With four meetings to go, it looked like it would go right to the wire between me and Lundy because I was only sixty-four points behind. At the next meeting, the final tarmac meeting of the season, I won two heats and the Grand National and finished second in the final to Andy Smith. That closed the gap at the top to less than forty points.

Shale was definitely my weaker surface in 1995, so I was worried that the last three meetings – Coventry, Stoke and Long Eaton – would see me struggle to compete with John. If I was going to outscore him by those forty crucial points, I needed to stop him finishing. I managed that at Coventry – he didn't finish the final with a flat tyre – but the trouble was that I didn't too, while Andy Smith took the win. Nor did I finish the Grand National, but John managed seventh. The gap between us increased a little and now there were only two meetings to go.

At Stoke, I was determined to try again. Neither John nor I qualified from our heats so we ended up in the consolation, but he got away to win it. Things were getting desperate. Finally, a proper chance came in the final. After a few laps, I found myself looking the Lund back bumper going into a corner. It was now or never. I rifled him towards the fence, making sure I shoved with enough power that he would go into the fence and not come out. Sure enough, he had to sit out the rest of the race while I finished third, behind Andy Smith and Phil Smith.

John Lund had the same idea as I did, though – his best chance to win was to stop me finishing. His mechanics did a great job getting his car back out on grid for the Grand National since both axles needed attention. But he wasn't there to race. As soon as the green flag dropped John put me on a fence post on the first lap – ironically, the same fence post that he had been sat on earlier in the night. I retired and John followed me onto the infield – he knew that his car wasn't in a fit state to race and he'd done what he needed to.

While neither of us finished, Andy Smith raced to second place from a lap handicap. He had won three finals in three meetings and, without Lundy or I really noticing, had been heaping loads of points together. Going into the last meeting of the season at Long Eaton, it had switched from a two-horse race to a three-horse race – and the horse in the lead going into the final gallop was Andy!

All three of us were drawn in the same heat at Long Eaton, which was probably fairer than having two in one heat and one driver in another. Especially when I was the one who won the race! Going into the final, it was still all to play for. Halfway through the final, it looked like the fairy tale was going to come true. I worked my way into the lead and was circulating with Peter Falding on my tail. But then Andy Smith clattered Peter from behind, pushing us both into the glue on the outside of the track. Andy got through to take the lead and, by the time I got back on the racing line, he was long gone.

I'll admit that I lost my rag a bit at this point. When John Lund came past, in desperation I tried to take him out, even though I knew it wouldn't really make any difference. Moves made in desperation often don't work out, and the only car that ended up in the fence was my own.

So Andy Smith ended up wearing the silver roof for the next year, John Lund finished second in the National Points, I was third. The top three drivers had fought it out over the whole season and it ended up in a great climax. Now that's how to decide who the best driver is!

John Goodhall – one of stock car's great characters,
lost to us in an accident I'll never forget

10

Three laps to go and I'm in the middle of a ding-dong battle for fifth place. A gaggle of red tops are roaring around the track, doing our best to catch the lower graders in front, but truth be told we're holding ourselves up rather than concentrating on catching those in front. It's been like that all night – the heats were all taken by blue and yellow tops, the best I could manage was sixth.

I floor the accelerator and roar out of the turn and onto the home straight. The cars in front of me – John Lund, Rob Cowley, Paul Harrison and John Cayzer – jink to the left or right. I'm the final one of the pack so I can't see what's up ahead. Suddenly a car appears in front of me, sideways across the middle of the track.

I don't have anywhere to go. I jam the brakes and try to turn the wheel but it's just too late. I hit the car in front.

Stock car racing is all about contact. I must have hit or been hit millions of times in my driving career. But no matter how long I race for, no matter how long I live, I'll never forget that impact.

Everybody who gets into a stock car and drives out on track knows that it is dangerous. They are literally risking their lives. I'd had my fair share of injuries since starting racing, but thankfully nothing too serious. The most time I'd spent out of the driver's seat was due to a broken arm, which was actually the result of a road traffic accident, not a stock car crash. But the dangers of stock car racing were brought home to me on 1 July 1995. It was just a regular Coventry meeting, one in which I'd struggled to get to the front of the pack. I wasn't the only one. John Lund, Paul Harrison and Andy Smith all crept into the final in fourth fifth, sixth and seventh place respectively in their heats.

I was hanging onto the back of the charging red tops in the final, knowing that I was racing for a place on the podium at best. A quarter-lap or so in front, John Goodhall was battling to retain fourth place. When John Wright went to overtake him, Goodhall – the wily old veteran – spun Wright in the corner, but he lost control of his own car a little and clipped the fence at the start of the home straight. He came to rest sideways on in the middle of the track. I was totally unsighted because of the cars in front of me and couldn't avoid hitting him side-on.

It was a racing incident, it was nobody's fault. After the race was stopped, I got out and went across to see John. With hindsight, I don't know whether that was the best thing for me to have done or not. I could tell that it wasn't good.

The race was called and the rest of the meeting was cancelled as the paramedics took John from his car and rushed him to hospital, but the signs were not positive. To put it bluntly, he was already dead, but they were waiting until they got to him to hospital to declare him so.

It hit me hard. I had just killed somebody.

John Goodhall died on Saturday night. The following day saw an afternoon meeting at Hednesford. I didn't want to race – I wasn't in the right place mentally and I was in agony physically after the big impact – but Peter Falding took me to one side and told me to get on with it. Essentially he told me that I couldn't change what had happened, so I just needed to suck it up and go back out there to do what I do best – race and entertain the fans, just like John did for over thirty years. It was a bit of tough love, but it was a conversation that I'll always appreciate Peter for. He knew, and my dad knew, that I needed to jump back on the horse. If I hadn't have raced I'd have sunk deeper into dwelling on it, and that wouldn't have helped anybody.

It was naturally a sombre meeting at Hednesford as news travelled around the pits and the stands that John Goodhall had died. This was before the internet, social media and mobile phones; news travelled slowly but gradually filtered through to everybody. I just went round and round, I wasn't interested in racing or in taking any risks.

The investigation into what happened hung over me for weeks and months afterwards. The car I was driving at Coventry had to be put to one side and investigators came up to the farm to examine it. I had to make a statement about what happened, as did many other people who were involved. Everything was logged and no stone was left unturned, quite rightly, because somebody had died.

But it was a stressful time. I could be up for murder. I knew that I hadn't done anything wrong, that it was a racing incident, but ultimately it wasn't my call. What if the investigators and the police didn't agree? I thought about that for a long time afterwards. Thankfully, John Goodhall's own family and mechanics were very supportive and helped get me through it. If they had pointed the finger at me in their grief, it would have made things so much worse.

A lot of things came to light in the investigation, things that could be improved to help with driver safety. Goodhall's seat and belts were hardly top-notch and he wasn't strapped in as well as he could be. When I hit the side of his car, he moved around so much that he broke his neck. There was nothing right about the safety in his cab.

That's when I decided to get properly involved with the drivers' committee. I threw myself into the safety aspect of the sport, trying to make sure that it didn't happen again. By the start of the 1996 season, two new regulations were introduced as a direct result of the Goodhall accident. First, a head restraint net had to be put in place to try to stop major whiplash injuries; second, all front bumpers had to include an under-bumper hoop to try to stop cars riding up and damaging the cab in a side-on impact.

Those two new regulations may have saved John Goodhall's life, they may not, but they were a forward step. The one piece of equipment that probably would have made a difference was a HANS device, a carbon-fibre head restraint that attaches to the helmet, but they were only just creeping into motorsport and hadn't yet been seen on a stock car track. The 'other' F1 only made HANS devices mandatory in 2003, NASCAR in 2001 and drag racing in 2004, so to expect amateur stock car drivers to have invested in them in 1995 is pretty unrealistic. But I'm pleased that HANS devices are now mandatory in stock car racing, as are fireproof clothing, improved harnesses and a host of other new safety enhancements.

Technology improves over time. It's interesting that, in the twenty or so years between when Brian Wallace died at White City in 1976 and John Goodhall died at Coventry in 1995, car building changed immeasurably. Look up an old photo of one of Brian Wallace's cars – or any of the cars driven that season – and compare it with John Goodhall's car, or one of mine from 1995, or any others on track that year. The 1995 cars look much more substantial. They look like a modern stock car rather than something knocked together by an amateur in a shed.

Then compare the 1995 cars with a modern car, another twenty or so years later. Cosmetically, they don't look all that different, but look deeper and you'll see that things have continued to improve – new and better regulations about the car and cab design, the type of steel used, the positioning of certain components.

Between the deaths of Brian Wallace and John Goodhall, we also lost Richie Ahern in 1983 due to complications after his accident in 1981, and Steve Froggatt, who never regained consciousness after a crash at Bradford in 1984. Thankfully, in more than two decades since John

Goodhall died, there hasn't been a single F1 fatality in the UK. By no means was I the only person involved in improving safety around the turn of the millennium, but I like to think that I played a part.

We should never rest on our laurels. There have been fatalities in other forms of oval racing, notably Piet Keijzer in the Netherlands, Steve Newman in saloon stock cars and the particularly tragic death of eleven-year-old Keir Millar. But there have also been big accidents in F1 that, had they happened in past decades, could have been a whole lot worse: Peter Rees being knocked out at Northampton in 2011 and Dean Whitwell's fire at Ipswich in 2013 spring to mind. If there is more we can do to avoid any driver going through the torment that I did at that fateful Coventry meeting in 1995, we should do it – no questions asked.

A parade of some of the top drivers from the late nineties
– how many do you recognise?

11

I'm leading the World Final at Odsal Stadium, Bradford.

Yes, I've been here before.

I've done the hard work, overtaking Andy Smith and John Lund to take the lead, but John is still lurking ominously behind. I know he won't settle for second in the World Final, especially since he needs this one to equal Stuart Smith's record of six World titles.

I'm watching him closely and, as we go down the back straight, I sense that he's right on me. I dip the brake as we go into the corner and it seems to confuse him momentarily. John turns away and into the loose shale by the wall while I floor the accelerator and pull away again. It's not the textbook way to avoid a hit, but hey ho, it worked this time.

Lundy is still there and I'm still watching him but suddenly a different car appears in my peripheral vision. He slides across the front of me and I have nowhere to go. I hit him and jerk the steering wheel, going across the track and touching the fence on the outside. I'm still going, but all my speed has been wiped out.

There's nothing I can do to stop the all-gold 53 car from catching me on the next corner rocketing away after glancing past. So near and yet so far. Again.

Making changes to make the sport safer is one thing. Making changes for the sake of it is another.

Keeping control of the cost of stock car racing has been a debate that has been around almost since the first meeting. Long before I started racing, long before my dad started racing, some drivers started sourcing better cars fitted with custom-built parts. Even in the 1950s, some drivers thought that the sport was moving too far from its roots and becoming too expensive.

By the mid-nineties, the cost of racing was becoming something that threatened to drive the sport apart. I struggled on for a season after Tim Mann moved onto Eurocars but it was definitely hard to pay for everything. When Phoebe was born in early 1996, the belt strap had to be pulled a notch tighter. It was one thing for me and Sam to without to pay for racing, but I wasn't going to let my kid go without.

Thankfully, a new knight in shining armour appeared to act as my main sponsor. Tony Cole had raced in the past in Formula 2 and now supported a number of different drivers with his wallet – he started off with Mark Taylor in F2 and followed him into F1, then offered a bit of help to Richard Mason, Kev Smith, Len Wolfenden and

Bill Bullock. He told me he was interested in helping me out because he recognised that I was really determined, keen to win and I was prepared to dedicate my whole life to stock cars to do so. I think he respected that. And since I was finding the financial side of racing to be hard at the time, I welcomed him with open arms.

Tony helped out by funding what I've always struggled with my whole career: the engine. By now I was building some great cars, but how to power them was the problem. I wasn't a top engine builder and I had to pay somebody else to do that for me but, with Tony's help, we got a couple of decent Ian Whitworth engines and I was consistently back on the pace again.

In 1994 and 1995, the number of race wins and final wins I had dropped back slightly. After Tony came on board in 1996, they jumped back up again. I passed the chequered flag first on fifty-seven occasions in 1996 and did even better in 1997 with sixty-seven wins. That's the most I ever won in a single season and, given the way that the fixture list has changed since then, it's likely to always be the case.

Not surprisingly, I won the National Points Championship on both occasions, the start of a streak of fourteen seasons where I would top the grading list at the end of the season. After the silver roof went down to the final race of the final meeting in 1995, I won it by 200 points the next year from John Lund. The next year, I was so far clear that I'd as good as wrapped up the title by mid-season. John was second again, but the eventual gap was about 800 points.

Pushing for the points was my new motivation. I went into each season wanting to be the National Points Champion. Past experience had taught me that the winner of the silver roof, the driver won the most points in the season, was the best driver. The World Final was a one-off race. Yes, it's a spectacle and it works for what it is, but the Points Championship was about working all season, every race, to get your car back out and get racing.

It occasionally changed how I raced. If I was battling for a minor place with somebody who wasn't a rival in the points, it didn't matter too much if they beat me. I didn't want to tangle with them and take myself out only to allow somebody else to finish and earn more points. On that occasion it might be better to settle for a lower place. But if one of my silver roof rivals – at this stage, usually John Lund – was in a battle with me, I wouldn't back down. Every point or two that he earned by finishing a place in front could matter at the end of a season.

That said, it would never make me back off from trying to win a race. If I knew I was in with a chance for the chequered flag, I'd take it, even if it was just a heat or consolation. To prove that I wasn't settling for second, have a look at the statistics for 1996. John Lund won sixteen heats. I won forty-six – nearly three times as many. And 1997 was even better, with me getting fifty heat wins, more than three times that of John.

It was a period of my career that I really enjoyed. I had a decent set up and a good team around me. Samantha and Phoebe came to meetings too, so we had a really close-knit, family-oriented racing team. We always looked forward to Long Eaton meetings in particular because afterwards which we would stay at the house of Anita Bacon. She lived close by to the stadium, worked on the turnstiles and was dating Samantha's brother, Shane, at the time. We'd go racing, have a party back at her house and kip on her floor or in the bus afterwards – I was a bit younger and could cope with it better back then!

One morning after a Long Eaton meeting, Sam, Phoebe and I piled back onto the bus ready to drive to Hednesford. I started up the engine and went to turn on the radio – but there was no radio, just a gap where it should be. I turned round and shouted at a sleeping Chris Binns, who has always been the practical joker in the team, telling him to get the radio out of hiding. I could tell by the look on his face that he had nothing to do with it. On closer inspection it turned out that all the CDs were missing, so were a couple of bags. We'd been burgled, which was obviously a pain, but what made it worse was that Binnsy and a few others were asleep on the bus at the time. Not only that, but the burglars had opened the fridge and taken the sandwiches – even sorting through the sandwiches, because they left the corned beef ones behind – and all this was going on about three feet away from Binnsy's head!

Binnsy is great to have around. He's the joker of the team. He has been with me since the earliest days of my F1 career and is an encyclopaedia when it comes to knowing the history of my career and cars. I've raced and built so many that I always lose track of who has what and which car I used at any particular time, but you can rely on Binnsipedia to know the answer. He's still a crap security guard though!

My dog wasn't much better on the security front. From the mid-nineties until 2008 we were joined at every meeting by Kiwi. She certainly looked the part of a guard dog – a big Alsatian – but she didn't have the personality for it. I'd often see parents looking nervously at her in the pits. A few minutes later, their young children had usually enveloped Kiwi in a massive hug and were hanging off her neck. She was just that kind of a dog, really loving, and the fans loved her too. She'd often get Christmas presents, even from people who supposedly didn't like me!

One time we set off for a Saturday night meeting at Coventry and Kiwi took up her usual position between two back-to-back seats on the bus. We stopped off at Castle Tyres in Bingley to drop off some tyres that needed repairing and, as usual, Kiwi hopped off the bus and had a sniff around. We got back going again and, more than three hours later, were almost at the pit gate at Coventry when Binnsy piped up from the back: 'Where's Kiwi?' My heart sank.

I rang Castle Tyres, but they were shut. I managed to get hold of the owner who went down to have a look and found her, but my big fierce Alsatian took one look at him and ran away! I rang my grandad next, he also got in the car and drove there, but by then they was nowhere to be found. Sam and her brother missed the race meeting and drove back up north in Shane's car, searching all around Castle Tyres too. They didn't give up until midnight but still couldn't find her. I was distraught, so after the meeting I borrowed a car and drove back home too, stopping off at Castle Tyres in the early hours of the morning, but still no sign of her.

The next day saw a meeting at Wimbledon so the rest of the team stayed down at Coventry with the bus and the stock car. I got up at 6.30 in the morning and drove straight back to Castle Tyres to have a look in the daylight. I turned into the industrial estate, followed the road down to Castle Tyres and spotted Kiwi, asleep in a big flowerpot right outside Castle Tyres! She sat up, looked at me and jumped in the car, as happy as anything. That day was my twenty-fifth birthday and I couldn't have had a better present than finding my beloved dog safe and sound. Sam and I drove down to Wimbledon and, just to add to how great I felt, I won both heats and the final despite only having about three hours of kip!

A year or two after her disappearing act, Kiwi must have snuck away again for a little bit, because a little while later we realised that she was pregnant. We took her to the vet and they confirmed that she was pregnant and offered to do an ultrasound for £30. Sam wanted to know how many pups Kiwi was having so she could start finding out some homes for the pups when they came, so I reluctantly handed my £30 over. The vet said there were definitely two pups, maybe three, possibly four. A few weeks later, we were on the bus on the way to a meeting and Kiwi started to get unsettled. We realised that she was about to have the pups while we were on the road. She lay down on the bunk, so we left her to it and Sam gave me a running commentary while I drove the bus. Pup number one arrived, then number two. 'There's three!' Sam called out. 'Now there's another one. That's four!' she said after a pause. Then, 'Five! There's a fifth. The vet missed one!'

By the time we got to Skegness, Kiwi had given birth to thirteen pups. Thirteen! One was obviously struggling and we ended up with the Skegness stadium paramedics on the bus unsuccessfully trying to revive a blue pup with a straw. People were waiting outside the bus, not to see the stock car, but to find out how the dog was. I just couldn't believe how useless the vet was. I paid £30 to have an ultrasound on which they'd missed nine pups. That's thirty-six legs! How did they miss all those? Sam tells me that it happened twenty years ago now and I've got to let it go, but I still begrudge that £30!

The trips on the bus were great fun, but another reason why I enjoyed racing in the second half of the nineties so much was that I took a few steps forward in terms of the World Final. The 1996 race saw me finally make the podium in my ninth full season of racing. I wasn't ever close to stepping up a place or two as John Lund and Paul Harrison charged off into the distance at Coventry, leaving me scrapping for third with Matt Bennett. By the time I was secure in that position, it was way too much distance to make up to Paul and John, but I was just happy to make the podium.

Tony Cole probably wasn't though. My improving results showed that his sponsorship definitely helped but he wasn't always the easiest of people to work with. He was so keen on stock cars and so keen to see me win that he actually became a bit of a pain. The money he gave me was helpful but opening up his wallet didn't give him a place in my life, and it seemed that's how it was going. He'd travel up from Sheffield to Silsden nearly every night to help out with the car. Sam would cook him some dinner and he'd spend the whole evening with us – it was like he was becoming part of the family. Eventually, it began to grate. Sam and I started to go out together on Wednesday evenings for a bit of freedom – we'd go out for dinner, to the cinema, something like that. But Tony wasn't keen – it was almost like he was jealous. He'd try to wangle his way in to join us for dinner. On one occasion, Tony set up an evening with some young offenders in Bradford. I was invited to take my car along and fire it up, chat to them and try to show them there were hobbies they could get involved with that would take them away from a life of crime. Tony insisted that the young offenders' group only met on Wednesdays. When I arrived, the organiser of the group welcomed me and said that the lads were really keen to meet me – so much so that they were expecting full attendance, even though it was an extra session because they never usually met on a Wednesday. It was all a ruse to get me out of date night with Sam.

Don't get me wrong, Tony could be a nice, polite chap and we had some good times, especially in 1996 and 1997, but he could be difficult too. It was almost like he was too obsessed with stock cars – and this is coming from me! Nothing was ever good enough for him. The final straw came when we were travelling back from the British Championship at Coventry in 1998. I'd qualified on pole after winning both my heats and ended up finishing second to John Lund. I missed a gear at the start and, although I made up most of the ground, somebody took my front shock absorber off. On the bus on the way home, Tony was ranting about the result. I was happy – I finished second in the British Championship with a car with no shocker on – but he was having a paddy. I ended up going to bed in a bunk at the back of the bus to avoid him but, when we stopped at the services, the other guys woke me up and said that he was still going off on one. Tony and I ended up having words and, ultimately, the bus left the services without him. It sounds harsh, but I ended up having to take a stand. Needless to say, the sponsorship dried up after that!

It was a real shame. I appreciated the sponsorship and I enjoyed the good times but it was like a competition for my attention, and I didn't like that Tony seemed to be stepping between me and Sam, especially after Phoebe came along. After that, I decided that I needed to rely on outside help less and I started funded my own racing a lot more. Tony had bought engines from Ian Whitworth for me to use. After Tony, I just went to Ian direct.

The financial side of F1 wasn't something that only I had to deal with. Things reached a head in the wider sport in 1997 when Gaz Bott unveiled his plan to launch a breakaway class of supermodifieds. Gaz was one of the drivers who had embraced the changes of the last few years – inside weight, Hoosier tyres and the like – which had made tarmac racing a much more specialised affair. Gone were the days of the one-car driver who could be competitive on both tarmac and shale. But Gaz was also frustrated with what he saw as the inability of the groups invested in F1 stock car racing – the promoters and the drivers in particular – to work together. He had a point. By the time Gaz made his announcement in April 1997, we still didn't have a confirmed venue for that year's World Final.

Gaz wanted a new tarmac-only formula which would race in a limited number of meetings to create a new series. He was thinking big. He wanted TV coverage, big corporate sponsorship and merchandise deals. He wanted a slick, commercial organisation. The drivers would be professionalised, with expenses covered and their own big-money sponsorship deals. But there were plenty who were against the plans. Many pulled out the old phrase 'that's not stock car racing'. Some were suspicious that Gaz wanted to become a Bernie Ecclestone-style supremo of oval racing.

Personally, I thought it was a non-starter. It's not what people wanted to see. They wanted to see a lot of cars on track, racing and competing, not just a handful going round and round. Stock car racing is what stock car racing is, it will never change or alter. As long as the people in charge keep it like it is; it will do okay. If the people in charge try to introduce fancy new tyres and engines that cost too much, it will die. The drivers won't feel like they can compete, they need an even keel. I'm a great believer that if it ain't broke, don't fix it; and I don't think that our sport is broke.

The fallout from the supermodified plans meant that Gaz Bott walked away from F1 after his World Semi-Final and didn't grid in the World Final, which was eventually confirmed as being at Bradford. It was the first time the race had been held there since 1994, the race where I conked out after being in the lead for so long.

The front row was John Lund and Andy Smith. I started on the inside of the second row. As far as the gold roof was concerned, we were the only cars in it. The three of us got away in a clean start with John pulling a bit of a gap while Andy and I battled for second. After six laps or so, I saw a chance to dispose of Andy when we lapped Rob Cowley. I managed to hit Andy wide, forcing him to go round the outside of car 73, while I nipped up the inside. Even better, Andy ended up with a puncture and retired.

After another six laps, I closed the gap to John and took the lead with a clean hit that put him wide and gave me time to get up the inside. I was in the lead, but almost immediately the race was yellow flagged so Henk-Jan Ronitz could be checked over by the medical staff. I kept the lead on the restart and opened up a bit of a gap, but I was well aware of Lundy in my rear mirror. I was watching him closely so I survived his first attempt to overtake, but I was watching him so closely that I was caught napping when Dutchman Benny Nauta crossed over the racing line as he tried to get to the safety of the centre.

And that was my chance gone. With only five laps to go, John sailed past, although both of us must have panicked slightly when we momentarily caught up our wheels. Once he had his nose in front, I didn't have enough in the tank to catch him again.

Third in 1996, second in 1997... one better in 1998?

The 1998 World Final – on the top step at last!

12

I'm back for another crack at the World Final. We're in Coventry and I'm starting on the outside of the front row, with John Lund on pole. As always, I fancy my chances. But as always, it's just one race and anything can happen.

Lundy controls the pace on the rolling lap and, as we approached the home straight, he puts the power on. We roar down the home straight but Chris Lloyd loses control on the inside of the second row and starts to spin. I have to edge a little wider into the corner, allowing John to go off unchallenged. Others sneak down the inside: Andy Smith, Rob Pearce and Paul Harrison. Before I know it, I'm going down the back straight in fifth.

What a crap start. If it's anything like past races, John will be off into the distance and I'll be fighting for a place on the podium again.

You know the drill. There's always next year...

But it wasn't like past races this time. In 1998, after what seemed like a lifetime of waiting (it was actually eleven years) I finally won the World Final. Here's how it came about.

Just making the grid at the Birmingham semi-final was an achievement. I'd blown up the engine in the tarmac car during the European Championship, only two weeks before the semi, and the big-block engine I had was also damaged. I'd parted company with Tony Cole a couple of months before and we weren't exactly on best terms for a few weeks, so I wouldn't have any help from that avenue. All I could do was work my gut off to get the small-block engine fixed and back in the tarmac car. Thankfully I did and drove to a fairly easy victory. The other big guns – Lund, Paul Harrison and Andy Smith – were in the other half of the draw.

Between the semi-final and the World Final I had a huge boost when I won the last ever World Long Track title at Baarlo. I'd now won the Dutch version of the World Championship and the New Zealand version of the World Championship. Why was it so damn difficult to win my own British version?

I didn't make things easy for myself by deciding to race at Coventry in my tarmac car, the one that won the World Long Track four weeks before. Stan Hickey was over from New Zealand and racing my old shale car, one that he had used in the Bradford World Final the year before when I finished second. The car that I used that day, my current shale car, was going to run in the World Final too, but not driven by me. That was promised to my brother-in-law,

Shane Dorrell, who had used it on tarmac in the Birmingham semi-final and now held onto it for the big race.

So that left me with the tarmac car. It was quick but not designed for shale. Using it in the World Final was a gamble but I didn't want to go back on my word with Stan and Shane, so it was either use the tarmac car or borrow one from elsewhere. I tried it out at Coventry two weeks before the World Final meeting and it went pretty well – I won the final and got fifth and second in two heats.

After an awful start, it looked like it didn't matter which car I was using, yet again I wasn't going to win the World Final. Lundy was streaking off down the back straight in the lead while I was fighting in the pack, having dropped back to fifth. But then everything seemed to come good.

I managed to get past Paul Harrison and Rob Pearce and was picking my way through a busy track. Cars were spinning all over and it was quite an effort just to avoid everybody and stay out of trouble. Five laps in, I was still minding my own business in third when, up front, John Lund got into a bit of trouble with two backmarkers. As he tried to escape them, Stan Hickey hit him hard. It damaged Lund's car to the extent that all he could do was limp onto the centre. No third time in a row for him.

Cue controversy number one. Of course, I ended up winning the race. Everybody knew that I was friends with Stan Hickey, that Stan was driving one of my cars, and that he was from New Zealand, which has a long history of team racing. Therefore, a lot of people assumed that Stan deliberately took out John so I could win.

It's a great story, but I'm as certain as I can be that it didn't happen. I can't say I'm 100% sure, because only

Stan knows what he did, but he has never owned up to taking Lund out on purpose and I'm pretty sure he would have told me by now if he had. Instead, Stan was just a little clumsy. He got hooked up on John and they tangled or something, that's all. And remember, it was a mad first few laps to that World Final. Cars were spinning out all over the place and it was an effort just to keep going. Stan wouldn't have known that John was leading and I was stuck in third place.

With John and Stan in the middle of the track at the start of the back straight, the next few cars came towards them: Andy Smith, Rob Pearce and me. Andy stuck close to the inside while Rob belted to the outside. I had nowhere to go, so I turned sharply. A nudge from behind sent me over kerb and onto the edge of the infield, so I stayed on there for the back straight and rejoined on the next corner, but I didn't have an angle to turn and ended up T-boning Andy Smith into Andy Robinson. Smith's car went up on two wheels briefly and came back down heavily. A bit like Lund, all he could do was creep to the infield. The impact helped me make the turn and I went off down the home straight in the lead.

Time for controversy number two. According to many, especially Smith supporters, I deliberately cut the corner and took Andy out.

Where else could I go? The track was blocked and it wasn't as though I choose to take the exact line I did – a different car knocked me onto the infield. And although I can't say for certain what Stan was thinking, I can tell you what I was thinking. I didn't deliberately ram Andy. It's stock car racing. It happens.

And that's pretty much the story of the 1998 World Final. After six laps, I was in the lead and never again touched. Rob Pearce carried on for second place, Paul Harrison for third, but for the first time I was the BriSCA Champion of the World.

I know I've made plenty of the fact that the National Points Champion is the best driver in stock cars, at least when the National Points Champion was the driver who won the most points over the course of the season. But there's no doubt that, when I was on the grid in the World Final, I still wanted to win it. And did it feel good to do so? Of course it did! It was a great feeling to know that I'd finally done it and proved the doubters wrong. To stick two fingers up to the people who called me the bridesmaid, who said that I couldn't perform in a big race when the pressure was on. I was now the only driver to have won all three World Championships in the countries that we race in, and I'd won all three over a period of just eighteen months. It was great for all my sponsors, both past and present, my family, and my hard-working crew.

There was a bit of a sour taste when I found out that there was going to be an official protest lodged at the re-sult – I don't think I'd even left the track before I was told. Two and a half weeks later, the disciplinary board met and considered the protests, which had been lodged by Rob Pearce and Andy Smith. They said that I deliberately cut the corner. According to their version of events, I wasn't the World Champion because I only completed twenty-four and three-quarter laps, not twenty-five.

Of course, I went along to the hearing to defend myself. Rob Pearce was there too but Andy Smith didn't bother to attend. I was confident that the board would hear in my favour and, after hearing the arguments and watching the video, they found that I had no case to answer.

Rob looked sheepish was very apologetic afterwards. I got the impression that he was persuaded to put the protest in by Andy Smith. After all, it gave the protest more gravitas because Rob was the driver who finished second and could conceivably gain from me being disqualified or docked, whereas Andy Smith had nothing to gain – it was just sour grapes. But did Rob really want to become the World Champion in those circumstances? Being awarded the title two and a half weeks later by three guys on a disciplinary panel?

I decided that I was going to take number 1 to race under and had already started doing so before the disciplinary committee met. To me, it's a great thing if the World Champion races as number 1. I'd thought that ever since I'd gone to New Zealand, where every year the winner of the New Zealand Championship is awarded the number 1NZ. Not just that, but the other drivers on the podium are awarded 2NZ and 3NZ. The Kiwi drivers live for those numbers and are so proud of racing with them. I thought to myself, why don't we do that in the UK? Only Peter Falding had asked for number 1 up to now, when he won the World Final in 1993, but I decided that I would be the second. Hopefully I'd do the number proud.

One of the few times I got in front of Rob Speak during
the 2000 European Championship meeting – but at
least I was beaten by my own car!

13

For once I'm racing for a championship and I'm well clear of John Lund and Andy Smith. The usual suspects aren't going to stop me this time.

It's the European Championship and the grid is in grade order, meaning that I started at the back with Smith and Lund, but I got away early while they struggled at the back.

I make my way past the cars who started in front; first getting round Paul Harrison and Murray Harrison, then the blue roofs of drivers like Gary Utley and Steve Booth. Then it's the turn of the Dutch challengers, Bert Schaap and Durk Griedanus, and the sole white top, Dave Barry. With Mark Gilbank out of the way, I'm past most of the field.

But not all. One driver is still in front. Rob Speak. There's no way I'm going to catch him. His car is just too good. And you know what? I couldn't be happier about it.

Most years had a familiar pattern to them. I'd start the season early – I never understood why some drivers would wait until the first Coventry or whatever to make their first appearance – and take an early lead in the National Points Championship. Sometimes I'd have the Points title wrapped up by the middle of the season.

The driver in an often-distant second place was initially John Lund. We had some good fights, although unfortunately the allegations of team racing by me and my buddies against John which first surfaced in the 1998 World Final were kept going by my brothers-in-law, Shane and Clinton Dorrell. They just seemed to keep taking Lundy out of races. Shane did it in one of my shale cars at Swaffham, when he rammed John when he was in the fence. I wasn't happy at all about that and loaded up the car before Shane got into any more trouble. Luckily it was just a one-off. Shane had lost his rag about something and took it out on John, it was nothing personal.

Clinton was more of a handful. He took John out of a final at Coventry for no real reason then did the same again in the 1999 British Championship final. But Clinton was acting completely off his own back. I didn't ask him to do it, nor did I need him to – I was comfortably winning races without his help. It put Sam in an awkward position too because everybody assumed that she had something to do with it. I tried to step in when I could – once putting my car between Clinton and John when Clinton deliberately lined up right behind him – but if he had set his mind on destroying John for some reason, I couldn't stop him.

Anyway, the rivalry between me and John began to tail off at the turn of the millennium. When foot-and-mouth disease caused him to miss a lot of 2001, he never got back up to challenging for the Points title again. Although out paths would continue to cross, we were no longer fighting to be top dog.

John's place was taken by another familiar rival, Andy Smith, who finished second in 1999 and 2000. He was still quite far back though. Such was my domination that I think I was on top in every grading period from the first regrading of 1996 (when I took over from Andy, who had won the silver roof in the last race of 1995) to the first regrading of 2001 (when Andy also took the lead, albeit only for one month before I got it back again).

There was a new name in the mix, though, and he would go on to finish second in the points in 2001. He also came very close to nicking first place in the first re-grading of 2000. And although he was a new driver to F1, I knew him pretty well from the past. His name was Rob Speak.

Rob came into F1 after dominating F2 for years and years, a situation similar to how I was doing in Formula 1. He'd win the Points Championship early on in the season, nobody else had a chance of catching him, but he also managed to do something that evaded me and get a whole collection of World Final wins too. Rob got a bit fed up of F2 at the end of the nineties and I think F2 got a bit fed up of him. So he threw his hat into the Formula 1 ring and, with the help of Jamie Davidson, tried to knock me off my perch.

That first regrading of 2000 saw me just cling on to top spot; I had 128 points from five meetings, Rob had 125 points from the same amount. So the signs were certainly there that Rob was going to give it his all in F1, and that was welcome. Every sport needs new blood to liven things up. For the last ten years, Formula 1 stock cars had basically been about Frankie Wainman Junior against John Lund with the occasional input from Andy Smith and Peter Falding. Things can sometimes become a little stale.

Rob is up front. What you see is what you get. He's not afraid to share his opinion. I had always got on with him and I helped him when he first started in F1. He targeted me on track, but I had no problem with that. It's part of stock car racing. Rob saw me as the top driver and wanted to make a statement by taking me on. If anything, I was flattered by the fact that he had a go at me rather than John Lund.

It started to go wrong when others got involved with Rob. He always had the talent but suddenly he had a bit of money backing him. The only trouble was it appeared that those backers wanted to get too involved: telling him who his rivals were, encouraging him to take people out, allowing the rivalry to build instead of leaving it where it belongs, on the track.

Where Rob did struggle when he first came into Formula 1 was with his cars. He just didn't have the right ones to start with. Eventually he came to me and asked me to build him a new car. At first, I wasn't convinced – not that I didn't want to, but I was just too busy. I'd just finished cars for Rob Perry and Ivan Pritchard, I was building a new tarmac car of my own that I was still working on in the middle of the season, and I already had a full order book for the next few months. But then I had an idea. I'd built and delivered a rolling chassis to Paul Higgins but he hadn't got around to doing anything with it yet. He said that he wasn't intending to race until the following year. Even so, he wasn't sure about handing back his half-complete car. After a bit of persuasion, which included a promise from me that he would get another rolling chassis during the winter and presumably a few notes from Jamie Davidson's wallet, Paul gave the car to Rob. He and his crew then had ten days to put an engine in it and get it ready to race.

Straight away, the car won during its first weekend, and it wasn't just any old race, but the European Championship in 2000. I came second – my own machine had prevented me taking a title. Did I feel bad? Not at all, it felt great!

Building a car for one of my competitors wasn't anything unusual. I'd been building cars for years – longer, in fact, than I'd been driving them! I first built a car for my dad, then I built my own cars when I started racing. When I built myself a new car, I'd sell on the old one to help fund the new one. After finishing my apprenticeship and leaving Landis Lund, I moved into building stock cars as a full-time job. That's when I started churning out car after car. At one stage, you could have made up a whole grid of top drivers in top cars, all Wainman-built. There were certainly plenty of occasions when I was denied a race win by one of my own cars.

So how do you build a stock car? It's not rocket science, although some builders try to make out that it is. Stock cars are quite basic machines. It has to go to the end of a straight, it has to stop and it has to turn. No matter what you do, they all have to have a certain amount of stuff in them to do that. It won't go round a corner quick unless you have five inches of stagger on it. There are no huge differences, no real tricks.

You start with two lengths of steel for the chassis legs and go from there. I have a flat jig that dates back to when I used to build cars with my dad. I think he first used it in 1978 to square his cars up and keep them dead true, then he copied the same design afterwards by lining the metal up in exactly the same place. Cars have obviously altered a lot since then and nothing on the jig actually lines up to anything now, the cross bars are all in different places now since I've altered them to my own design, but I still use it to put the steel on and keep it square and flat. Now I build so many cars in a year that I get the jig down, lay four or five different cars out and stack them up.

If you want to recognise a Wainman car, look at the pipework. I like it to be neat. I think it goes back to my days as a pipe fitter for Landis Lund. Sometimes the pipes in my cab take me days to get just right but nobody else will ever see them. It's just something I have to do right.

Over the years you learn things and develop a particular style. My cars are strong, I've worked out how to make them last. One thing I learned from going for the Points Championship is that my car had to do every race at every meeting. For that to be possible the car had to have a strong structure and have bits on it that were tough. Yes, the back axle might be fifteen kilograms heavier than somebody else's, but it would do all four races at a meeting while their car was back in the bus because it broke. And that's how it has always been, even with my customer cars. As a car builder, you might say that my cars are too strong and they last too long. Business-wise, that's probably not a good thing. They should be like a Tom Harris car, which lasts a couple of years before it falls apart. Then you can build another one and charge them another fifty grand or whatever. I did start using space frames for a while after seeing them in New Zealand, but they were way too strong and were starting to hurt drivers. There was no give on them.

You also have to learn to evolve and develop with the rules. One of my best cars was the tarmac car I raced in 1995. It was the time when they first introduced weight distribution and you could only have 52% of the weight on the inside, so I built this one and started the season with five consecutive final wins on tarmac. It was a time when I was racing without a major sponsor so I didn't have a decent engine, but I still managed to win because I had a car with awesome chassis handling. I didn't have lots of cash, but I did have knowledge and expertise so I was the first one to get to grips with the new regulations. When they altered the rules on weight distribution again, we had to move the engine about and it messed up the handling of the car. It was never as quick again, so I had to develop something else. The result was the little black car – that also dominated for a couple of years and won the Long Track Championship and World Final, until the rules changed yet again.

Changing with the rules is one thing, but back in the day a few people cheated with stuff. I was often up against people who were running dodgy gear, but I knew they had it. So I took a step back and waited until they take it out. When the playing field is level again, it's all okay.

Over the years I've tried a lot of things. Look around a car and you'll see little things that can be tinkered with. Suspension designs: I've had them all on. I had a four-link rear suspension on in 1990. I didn't particularly understand it very much then, but now I have it on again. I was one of the first to put coilovers on the front instead of leaf springs. They took a bit of messing about to get sorted, but I got there with it. I looked at what was being done in the USA and New Zealand and tried things out. I still do – my most recent shale car had a few bits and pieces on it that were inspired by things I'd seen in New Zealand.

Once, when I built Paul Harrison a new tarmac car, it was better than mine because it had a better engine. Paul could afford it and he won heat and final straight away in it as a result. That's just how it is and I wouldn't have it any other way. I've heard horror stories about people building cars and not doing a proper job because it's for somebody else. What's that all about? If you are building cars, you are building cars. It happened to me too, when Clive Lintern threw together the car for Tim Mann because he heard I would be driving it and refused to help sort it afterwards. You'd never catch me doing that.

Of course, not all of my cars won the first time out. I remember building a car for Gaz Bott. He couldn't get it to go round the track and was moaning about it. At the end of the meeting we swapped cars, I went out in his and he went out in mine, and I absolutely whupped him. In his car. There was nothing wrong with it; he just couldn't drive it right. Once he learned to drive it, he was alright. I've always been good at being able to jump into any car. Because I've driven a lot of crap – and I have certainly driven a lot of crap – I can jump in any cars and still go out and win in it. Maybe you get it through experience. Other drivers don't have it and they have to be in their own car. But to me, a car is a car.

Part of the great thing about stock cars is that drivers help each other out in the pits, even if they are rivals. It's especially the case for the drivers who are also car builders. Watch me or Mat Newson in the pits at a meeting – we never stop. People are always coming to us for advice, or to buy or borrow a part, or to ask us to take a look at something. I help anybody who needs it, even top drivers. I remember helping Andy Smith during the first year he was the gold top. His tarmac car was crap and I swapped all the springs. I don't like to see people struggle when I know there's something I can do.

Not everybody is like that. Pete Dorrell once told me that he asked Stuart Smith what tyre pressures to run. Pete followed his advice but it didn't help at all. It was only when he got chatting to my dad that he was told he had completely the wrong set up. Stuart had told him a load of rubbish, presumably on purpose. To me, that's not being respectful.

The year after Rob Speak won the European Champion-ship in my car, we had the World Final at Hednes-ford. Rob Speak had moved on to a tarmac car built by Terry George at Elite, but it wasn't as good as he hoped. I chopped it up a little bit for him and helped him set it up for the World Final. What happened? Rob went and won. Had I not altered his car, he wouldn't have made the top ten. I finished in second place, having got the best of Andy Smith in a long battle for second which allowed Rob to streak away.

Yes, it was back to the same old story in World Finals after tasting success in 1998. The 2001 World Final which Rob won was the third in a row that I'd started on the outside of the front row with Andy Smith on pole (and the year before I started on the outside of the front row with John Lund on pole – so I was getting used to it!) In 2000, I lasted just over half a lap before getting spun by Ray Witts and hit by every car on the grid as they came past – at least, that's what it felt like. And in 1999, I was part of one of the most dramatic finishes in stock car history.

I'd started the race slowly, getting a bit stuck in the shale on the outside of the track, so Andy Smith, John Lund and Murray Harrison got past on the first corner. All I could do was plug away with consistent laps and I was rewarded when Murray spun after about six laps to move me into third, then Lundy spun to allow me into second. There then followed ten laps where I gradually closed the gap to Andy Smith. With five to go, I got up the inside to take the lead. But Andy wasn't going to let me past so easily – it was the World Final, after all. He kept trying to attack, I had to defend, and all the time John Lund was catching back up.

With two laps to go, everything happened at once. Andy made another attempt to overtake, bashed me wide and I started to spin. Then John Lund suddenly joined the party, running wide with both of us as he tried to latch onto Andy's back bumper. Before I could do anything, I was facing the wrong way with Andy blocking my route out of the fence and John trying to climb over my car and the fence at the same time. Andy and John had taken all three of us out of the battle for the lead. John got going again and crossed the line for third place, Andy crawled over the line in twelfth. The win went to Murray Harrison, who drove round the corner, spotted us in the fence and took the chequered flag unchallenged.

It was a tremendous finish that had everybody on the terraces leaping around with excitement, but I hoped that Samantha wasn't one of them – she was heavily pregnant with our second child. Less than a month later, he was born. Frankie (because what else was he going to be called?) missed his first weekend of racing, which is most unlike a Wainman, but given that he was born by an emergency caesarean section and only came home on the Friday, we'll let him off. The next weekend, mum was in the pits showing off her new son!

Within three months, little Frankie's dad was a World Champion again – I'd won the World 240 Championship in New Zealand for a second time. A few weeks after that, I was also a non-drinker.

If I'm honest, I was a crap drunk. Wherever you find stock car fans, mechanics and drivers, you'll always find plenty of beer, although obviously not when the drivers are behind the wheel. But I could put it away quickly when the meeting finished, in the bar or on the bus or wherever the next party was. So I was used to drinking plenty, but I could be a bit of a dick with it.

After winning the World 240 title for the second time, we had a party in the village to celebrate. People came from all over to join in – it was a party and we're talking stock car people, after all! Ivan Pritchard turned up late and had his lorry with him, so he dropped it at the farm and I gave him a lift back down to the party. I sunk a lot of beers and, at the end of the night, found the car keys in my pocket. I decided I couldn't be bothered waiting for a taxi and decided to drive home.

It wasn't far but I still didn't make it. I crashed the car through a wall and had to be hauled home by other people. The next day, I was laid up in bed feeling sorry for myself – I was hungover, I'd trashed the car and I was a little sore. Mum turned up and gave me one of those looks that only mums can give. That made me feel even worse. I decided then that I wouldn't drink again and I haven't touched a drop since. All booze did was make me feel bad and made me act like an idiot. What if Phoebe or Frankie had been in the car with me?

Nobody believed I would be able to stop drinking. They were taking bets on when I'd start again, but I was determined. Once I got through those first couple of years, I was fine. It's hard work when everybody is drunk in the bar and you're trying to have a conversation with them, but it doesn't bother me in the slightest now. Since then, when I've won races and titles, I can remember everything. I don't miss it at all. Now my only vices are coffee and crashing cars – but only on the racetrack!

Testing the fence at Wimbledon courtesy of Rob Speak!

14

I'm defending my silver roof and the title is going down to the wire again, just like it did in 1995. Andy Smith is the one who is threatening to take it off me, just like he did seven years ago.

We're both racing in the final at Northampton, the penultimate tarmac meeting of the season, and we've both elected to play our jokers to earn double points. The race starts fine, but then I end up drifting onto the middle with car trouble courtesy of Rob Speak and the fence. Andy Smith circles the track for third place but must feel like he's won the World Final. Over the course of the season I've won twice as many heats and twice as many finals as he has and suddenly he's only a handful of points behind me in the National Series standings.

I've played my joker but all I'm left thinking is: this whole competition is a joke.

My entire life has revolved around Formula 1 stock cars. I grew up in a stock car family and I raced F1 as soon as I was old enough. I spent every evening building and repairing cars until I finished my apprenticeship, then I did it as a full-time job – which still involved me spending every evening building and repairing cars, it's just that I was doing it during the daytime as well!

So the decision I took in 2002 wasn't taken lightly. Not at all.

I decided to retire from Formula 1 stock cars. I wasn't going to race them. I wasn't going to build them. I was going to move to the other side of the world.

The reason? A decision taken by the BSCDA and BriSCA promoters which I still don't agree with. Over the winter between the 2001 and 2002 stock car seasons, it was decided that the National Points Championship, which had existed as long as the sport itself, was going to be replaced with something different: the National Series.

For forty-seven years, since stock car racing had started racing in the UK, drivers were graded according to the points they won at meetings. At the end of the season, these points were totted up and the overall leader was the National Points Champion. Initially they had two silver stripes on their roof; from 1982 they could paint their entire roof silver.

It's a simple format and it worked. Whoever won the National Points Championship had a reasonable claim to being the best driver in the sport. I'd found out the hard way that you need a good dollop of luck to win the World Final but, over the course of a full season, luck evens it-

self out. Cream rises to the top. The roll of honour for
the National Points Championship includes some great
names: Peter Falding, Bert Finnikin, Mike Close. Some of
the stars of the early days are there too: Johnny Brise, Fred
Mitchell, Doug and Alan Wardropper.

There are also some drivers who dominated the National Points Championship for longer periods. Stuart
Smith was the first. He won thirteen in a row. My dad
won three in a row, John Lund had six. And I had won the
National Points Championship every season since 1996.

And that was the problem. I'd had a silver roof (when
it wasn't gold) for six years and nobody was coming close
to beating me. To me, that showed that I was the best
driver in the sport. It was something that should be celebrated, but instead, certain people were getting fed up
with me winning it all the time. They couldn't beat me on
the track, so they tried to change the rules instead.

The National Series was raced for over thirty-five meetings although only the best thirty scores counted. Whoever scored the most points over those meetings would
now get to wear the silver roof. Drivers could score double
points in two meetings – one on shale, one or tarmac –
by announcing in advance that they were playing a joker.
There was a separate mini-series on tarmac only, there
were separate mini-series for the first and second halves
of the season, and there were mini-series for each grade.
It was way too complicated – presumably they had to get
Carol Vorderman to total the scores after each meeting.

The National Series was the idea of Stuart Milnes,
the BSCDA Chairman, who also happened to be a mechanic for Andy Smith. What a surprise. Lo and behold,

when the season started, Andy targeted the National Series meetings and didn't really bother with anything else. Somebody with a suspicious mind might think it was planned to benefit Andy all along.

With five meetings to go, Andy was getting pretty close. When we both played our tarmac joker at Northampton, he was the one who benefited – my battles with Rob Speak were a distraction and I didn't finish the final. Then following day, at Wimbledon, things got even worse.

I knew I was tweaking the tail of the dog when I put Rob in the fence in the final. Rob had announced he was quitting at the end of the season and had nothing to lose. I needed to collect some points to keep me ahead of Andy. So binning Rob probably wasn't the most sensible move, but I did it anyway.

We rolled out for the Grand National and I could tell that Rob's car was struggling. His back bumper was flapping – that should have been easy to fix – which meant that his crew were focusing on more serious things. The scrutineer has a close look at his car and passed it fit to race – a decision probably helped by the fact that he was out on the track examining the car and the crowd were getting on his back. They wanted to see Rob race, they wanted fireworks. Rob wasn't bothered that his car was in pieces – he only had one thing on his mind.

When the green flag fell, I pushed Rob from behind and got past. I expected him to struggle to keep control but he fought the car round the corner and pulled in behind me down the back straight. I should have hit him harder but I thought getting away from him would be easy. Now I knew what was coming. Time to grip the wheel and hope for the best.

His car got bigger and bigger in the mirror. I tried to turn the corner but Rob hadn't bothered to slow down – it turned out he had barely any brakes. Smack. Straight into a fence post. Both our races were over and Andy was able to take second in the Grand National with a decent points bonus after winning the final.

That allowed Andy into a nineteen-point lead in the National Series with three meetings to go but I soon got that back and finished ahead of him. It was close, but I took great pleasure in beating him at the end. The rules were altered to suit Andy and he still couldn't beat me. Maybe that contributed to his decision to not race F1 the following year.

I just didn't understand the logic of the National Series. I still don't. It's absolutely fine if you want invent a new championship, but why replace a championship which has existed for as long as the sport has? Why steal its roof status? All it would do was give the silver roof to somebody who didn't want to do the meetings, but I think that somebody who races week in, week out should have their commitment recognised. I finished nearly 500 points ahead of Andy in the grading points. So would it have been fair if he'd scraped a narrow win in the National Series and had the silver roof? I don't think so – it would have rewarded his decision to race less meetings. It got to the stage that I ended the 2004 season with 2021 points and the next-highest driver, Paul Harrison, had 882. All the National Series did was encourage top drivers to race less, not more.

Anyway, if the National Series was designed to give the silver roof to other drivers it was hardly a raging success. In the seven years that it existed in that format, I finished top of the now-obsolete grading points chart every year and won the National Series title and silver roof six times. It made bugger all difference. I still won.

The only time that I didn't, I got in trouble. In 2006, Andy Smith won the National Series. I turned up at the start of the 2007 season with a red roof (the first time in ten years) and 'National Points Champion' written on my car. Apparently that brought the sport into disrepute, but I was trying to make a point – there was no longer any recognition for the driver who won the most points in a season. That passed most people by at first because I was still winning the National Series and topping the grading points. But later on, when drivers like Tom Harris and Mat Newson started finishing on top of the points chart, people suddenly realised that they were getting nothing for it.

The fallout over the National Series led to both me and my dad leaving the BSCDA committee. We felt like they were changing the rules just because nobody could beat me. Of course, they denied that, but they would. To be honest, I was glad to get out. I've been asked back to the committee loads of times since but I think I've served my time. Time for somebody else to have a go.

Yet I was so pissed off with the entire situation that I nearly walked away from the entire sport, not just the committee. In 2002, Sam and I started the process of emigrating to New Zealand. We loved it there – we still do – after visiting a number of times to race superstocks. My brother-in-law, Shane, had just moved across, so we already had family there, and we had plenty of friends, including Stan and Sonja Hickey at Rotorua. The kids were still young enough – Phoebe was six, Frankie was two – that they'd settle in quickly and school shouldn't be a problem.

The plans progressed quickly. We found a plot of land and had designs drawn up for a house to be built. We had the finance in place and submitted all the paperwork. Being accepted into the country wasn't a problem, I had offers of work so we had the number of points needed. Only when it came to finally committing to the move did I have second thoughts. The main reason we didn't go was my family, in particular my grandparents. I couldn't leave them. I'd lived at the farm with my grandma and grandad next door for nearly all my life. I used to be in Grandma's house every single day. Now I was thinking about moving to the other side of the world and realistically I would never see them again. I wouldn't have been able to visit the UK every year because my financial situation would have been completely different. Drivers in New Zealand normally only visit Britain once during their career because it's so expensive and there isn't as much money in the sport over there. My grandad died in December 2004, so had we left in late 2002 as was the plan, I'd have missed the final two years of his life.

Looking back, I know we made the right call to stay, but that doesn't stop me wondering occasionally what life would have been like if we had moved. One thing is for sure – I'd have left Formula 1 stock cars after fifteen years. I'd have won the silver roof eight times, but I'd have only won the gold roof once.

I still had plenty more to do.

Plenty of fireworks after the 2005 World Final –
luckily for me, there weren't many during the race

15

I'm going to drive my car into the fence on the first turn.

As race strategies go, it's probably not the cleverest, but it's one that I think might work. I've got the quickest car on tarmac and everybody else knows that. Peter Falding will be keen to win his third World Final in a row and has been around long enough to know that he is going to have to play rough. Andy Smith seems to take great pleasure in stopping me winning the gold roof and he's in the best position to stop me.

So why don't I do their job for them? If I drive myself into the fence, at least I'll be the one in control. I can decide how quick I'll be going and what angle I'll hit it. If they are stupid enough to try and get on my tail, well, they'll be coming too.

It's a crazy idea. But it might just work...

Despite the best efforts of the BSCDA to stop me winning, I kept on picking up race wins and trophies. Aside from picking up the silver roof nearly every year, I became the most successful driver in British Championship history. John Lund had previously won six titles, I made it to seven. I'd already won it in 1992, then I added titles in 1999 and 2001 – both pretty easy wins at Coventry. Then I went on a streak of four in a row between 2003 and 2006. To win the British, you need to be a good all-round driver. You need to qualify from your two or three heats with solid, consistent finishes, but then you need to push on and go for the win in the championship race. Sometimes you need to adjust your car to suit the different approaches to heat and final. Sometimes the conditions can change over the course of the meeting as the temperature drops or if rain changes the track. Whatever the case, it's a championship format that seems to suit me.

The British may have been good for me but the World Championship was not. To be fair, it wasn't the whole of the World Championship process where I struggled. I'd usually do well in the qualifying meetings and finish top or second in the standings so I had pole position in one of the semi-finals. I'd make sure I qualified but most of the time I'd win and be on the front row of the World Final. That's when it would all go wrong.

I dropped back to fourth pretty quickly in the 2002 World Final and was just making my way back to the front, getting into second place, when I put a wheel on the concrete infield and my half shaft let go. Having one wheel gripping on concrete and the other wheel slipping on the Coventry shale isn't a recipe for success.

The following year was Coventry again and, unusually this time, I didn't start towards the front. I'd started my semi-final at Sheffield from pole position but didn't manage to finish the race. Early on I got sideways and Neil Scothern tried to drive over the top of me. I was forced to drop into the consolation semi-final which, luckily for me, was at Hednesford. The big tarmac oval there gave me plenty of time to catch the lower graders and I finished first – Neil Scothern was the other lucky loser.

Starting the World Final from the fifteenth row didn't give me much chance of success and I did about as well as I could to finish sixth, but at least I'd preserved my streak of qualifying for the World Final. When I lined up on the grid at Coventry in 2003, it was the thirteenth consecutive season that I'd qualified for the big race. That in itself was an achievement. I don't think Stuart Smith managed more than nine in a row, while even a driver with the longevity of Willie Harrison didn't race more than six in a row. So to be in double figures in terms of consecutive Word Finals was quite something.

I was back in the familiar surroundings of the front row in 2004, to the outside of pole-sitter Stuart Smith Junior. He led for the first few turns but I took over after three laps. It wasn't to last, though. Peter Falding was the quickest on track and bumpered me wide halfway through the race, which dropped me down to third. Then Stuart decided to try a big hit and we both rattled the fence. I don't really know why he did it because all he achieved was relegating me to tenth while he damaged his car and had to retire. My race was as good as over, although I did manage to overtake a few cars and ended up in fifth.

That was one of the first occasions I'd had a coming-together with Stuart. He was just starting out and I'm sure that he and all the Smith supporters hoped that he'd be just as strong a rival as his brother Andy had been for so many years. It hasn't really turned out that way. Yes, we've had the odd bit of bother here and there, but no more than any other top driver. Stuart is a good big-race performer but, unlike Andy, he has never been consistently at the top of the sport for long enough to keep appearing on my radar. Stuart and I also shared some good times together in New Zealand and our relationship has always stayed on the right side of respectful. He's still a driver I keep a wary eye on though!

Given my past failures, I hardly went into the 2005 World Final expecting to win, despite being back on pole position. There was a good omen the weekend before, however. The fixture list led to an odd situation where we raced at Northampton, the venue for the World Final, seven days before the big race. As you'd expect, plenty of drivers turned up to try set up their cars for the week after. However, I spent more time wandering around the pits on my phone, listening to my dad and Alison describe the Ministox National Championship at King's Lynn. I'd spent the last couple of years helping my little brother Danny with his Ministox, taking him to as many meetings as I could. Now he had a punt at winning his own gold roof.

Everything seemed to be going well and Danny was in the lead. Then, with about two laps to go, the phone went silent. It was awful – I kept shouting down the phone, trying to get a response and find out what was happening.

Then Alison's voice came back, saying that Danny had won. Everybody thought I'd won the lottery. I was jumping around like a madman. I was well happy for Danny, and my mood improved even more when I went out in my meeting and won the final. Suddenly everything was looking up.

I was in the same tarmac car that I'd raced for the last four years because it was still going well. Seven days later, on World Final day, I got to Northampton early and did about ten laps of practice. That was enough for me. I had set my car up the week before when the track was in the same condition as it would be during the World Final. The car was dialled in right and I knew I didn't need to do anything to it. Andy Smith, who was on the outside of the front row, spent about four hours trying to get his car set up. I watched him and his dad keep on trying new things to get it to go better, but I knew and they knew that the conditions would be different when the race came around. Spending so long practising was a sign of desperation. I knew that Andy was struggling and that only meant one thing. He was going to go after me early on, before I drove away from him.

He went for me, but I wasn't there to be had. On some occasions, I've hung back at the green flag to make sure I didn't get squashed against the wall. Not this time. I purposely put my foot to the floor and drove myself into the wall, knowing that it was the best way to make sure he couldn't destroy me. I knew that my car handled better so I could drive into the corner fast and turn hard. Andy had it all to do just to make contact. I don't think he touched me, certainly not enough to send me into the fence hard.

But he also had no chance of making the turn himself, so he hit the fence too.

It was a risk, but a very calculated risk. I knew my car was strong and I was in control the whole time. I simply bounced off the fence and rocketed off while Andy went backwards. By the time we reached the end of the back straight I had about a four car-length lead and I stayed in the lead from flag to flag to win the World Final for the second time. It might have been a boring race from the stands, but from the driver's seat it was one I enjoyed!

The first time I won the World Final, in 1998, Andy Smith cried foul to the stewards. This time he had no grounds to appeal. It was clear that I had won. I crossed the line way ahead of Dave Schaap. I had the fastest car and I out-thought everybody going into that crucial first corner.

At the time, I became the seventh driver to win multiple F1 World Finals. Andy Smith joined that club the following year at Coventry. I started from dead last on the grid, having failed to finish my semi-final at King's Lynn. Andy, meanwhile, was on the front row with John Lund. To have any chance of winning, I needed a few lots of yellow flags to bunch everybody up. You can almost guarantee race stoppages in a World Final. It's a packed, closed grid with all the top drivers, all on a similar pace, all charging into the first corner. Hardly surprising that fireworks are usually the result. And on this occasion? No bloody yellow flags. The entire race was run without a stoppage. Typical.

It's a pity, because I was on a charge too. I knew I might as well go for broke, so I went out hard. I couldn't afford to spend a lap or two sizing up each car in front, I had to deal with them quickly and move on to the next one. From thirty-first on the grid at the green flag, I was up to fifteenth on lap four – more than halfway through the field. By lap six, I was in ninth.

At half distance, I was fourth. Things slowed down a little after that as the lead cars became spread out, but with three laps to go, I got past Stuart Smith Junior and this time he didn't try to put me through the fence. And that's the way it stayed until the chequered flag. Thirty cars started in front of me and I finished in front of twenty-nine of them. If the race had been stopped, I might have defended my title and become a treble World Champion. It would still happen, but I'd have to wait another decade for that.

Taking the chequered flag in a soggy World Cup race
at Venray in 2006

16

Five laps to go? That's come round quick! I'd better get a move on, Second place is first loser.

I start to hold the accelerator for a little longer, press the brakes a little harder, turn the steering wheel a bit tighter. The time for conserving tyres is over.

The gap to blue-top Gary Castell closes quickly, like I've got him locked in a tractor beam. He must be looking in his mirror knowing that it's over.

One lap to go and I'm close enough to turn inside him and get down the straight to take the chequered flag in the first ever championship race at Venray. I must admit, I left that one a bit late!

When Baarlo closed at the end of 1998, the premier Dutch championship – the World Long Track – went with it. Although I was the final Long Track Champion, I would have the chance to defend my title, of sorts. Promoter Harry Maessen announced his intention to stage a new championship, initially known as the Euro Challenge Cup, at his own track at Venray.

It wasn't the Long Track – nothing else would ever come close to matching that – but it was a good enough replacement. Over the years, plenty of tracks have come and gone, both in the Netherlands and in the UK. The sport and its governing bodies just have to evolve to the new system and the World Cup (as it soon became known) went from strength to strength.

The inaugural Euro Challenge Cup was raced for in August, although the results of the previous meeting at Venray contributed to the positions on the grid. On championship day, two more heats were run to add to the May results, in which I finished second and third. That moved me up to the outside of the second row.

Ron Kroonder was in front of me on the outside of the front row – that was to be expected. But the driver on pole, who had won both heats earlier in the day, was more of a surprise. It was Gary Castell, a UK blue top who had returned to F1 after a short break and was starting to make a name for himself.

Before the race started we were told that it was going to be run over twenty-three laps. It seemed an odd number and I questioned it in the briefing, but we were told twenty-three it was. On the drop of the green, Castell powered off into the lead. I knew we were in for a long haul so settled in behind Kroonder in third place.

The gaps between us stabilised for the first half of the race. I knew I could push a little harder but I wanted to conserve my tyres. It's a difficult thing to do, to allow your opponents to get away, but sometimes you have to trust your instincts. After twelve or so laps, I slowly caught and passed Kroonder for second position, but Castell still held a good lead.

The lap boards came out a little earlier than I expected and I had to get a move on. I started to push harder. With three laps to go, the gap suddenly began to close. On the first turn of the last lap, I took a tight line on the inside and got through. Gary had pushed much harder in the first half of the race and his tyres had gone off – he just couldn't get round the corner as quick as I could, so I accelerated down the back straight with enough daylight between us to stop a last bender.

I'd defended my title by timing my race to absolute perfection – although it was actually a bit of an accident because it turns out that the chequered flag was waved on lap twenty, not lap twenty-three! Not that it made a huge difference because by the end of the race Gary was going backwards. Another three laps would have just increased my margin of victory, although it might have stopped me panicking when the lap boards first came out!

The conspiracy theorists must have had a field day. Not only did I nearly lose out because the race was flagged early, but I also nearly lost the title in the pits. I drove my car onto the scales and was told that it weighed 1268 kilograms. What? The limit was 1300, so I was well under and I knew that there was no way that the reading could be right. The figure was so far off that I knew something was wrong. We had a quick check around the car – nothing was missing, nothing had fallen off – so I pushed the car off the scales and asked to check them. The scrutineer was very reluctant to show me his display, but once I made him do so, it showed a weight of -54 when my car wasn't on scales. After a brief investigation, it turned out that they hadn't been set up properly. When the scales were zeroed, it turned out that somebody had 'accidentally' left their foot on one of the pads. When the scales were properly zeroed, I drove back onto them and they registered 1322 kilograms. I can't say that I was convinced by the scrutineer's explanation, but at least I hadn't been denied the win.

Maybe the Dutch were getting fed up of me winning their main title, because the following year I wasn't even allowed to race. I'd crossed the Channel in June to race in the Dutch Open at Venray, but I did so in Gary Utley's car because I was having problems with my own. I'd done really well, only to find out that I'd been disqualified on a technicality. I can't remember exactly what the problem was because getting to the Netherlands to find out that the Dutch had changed the rules yet again was a regular occurrence. What was more frustrating was that we were often only told about the rule changes after we'd fallen foul of them and been disqualified. It was distinctly suspicious and gave all the Brits – not just me – the impression that it was being done to stop us winning.

On this occasion, I lost my temper and drove my car around the track to give the promoter, Harry Maessen, a piece of my mind. It wasn't a pretty piece of diplomacy but I went away feeling happy that I'd got it off my chest.

Unfortunately, some of the Dutch contingent saw an opportunity to stop me winning three Long Track/World Cup championships in a row. A couple of days later, I was told that I'd been banned for one Venray meeting for trying to run over Harry Maessen! It was a load of rubbish and a complete overreaction. The real reason for the ban was revealed with a glance at the fixture list – the meeting that it covered just happened to be that year's World Cup.

I was back in 2001 and finished second to Henk-Jan Ronitz. Although I briefly got the lead, I didn't deal with Henk well enough and gave him a chance to retake first place. The following year I was second again, this time to future Formula 2 World Champion Willie Peeters – I actually crossed the line in third, but second-placed Sip Woudstra was eventually disqualified for having a problem with his rear tyre. Then in 2003 I got on the podium again, this time in third behind Ronitz and Woudstra.

Racing in the Netherlands was certainly something I was good at. If you ignore the year I was banned, I finished on the podium in six consecutive championships – the final two Long Tracks and the first four World Cups. That run finally came to an end in 2004 when Henk-Jan Ronitz won again. In second place on that occasion was Piet Keijzer. Piet had been around for longer than I had and was a top driver but always seemed to be the bridesmaid. Some drivers seem to struggle to win silverware but are always up there challenging: Mat Newson is one at the moment, Paul Harrison was the nearly man in World Finals for years, Dave Berresford spent years as a superstar without winning a gold or silver roof. Piet Keijzer was the same. He finished second in the Long Track in 1994 and second in the World Cup in 2004.

Unfortunately, he never would win it. I wasn't at the fateful World Cup meeting at Venray in 2005 where Piet lost his life, but by all accounts it was just a tragic accident. Piet had a flat tyre and was trying to get onto the infield when he got hit from behind and spun a few times. It didn't look anything too serious, but it quickly became clear that something was wrong and Piet was declared dead before the air ambulance could arrive.

I did, however, go over for the funeral. We took the car with us and I drove it as part of the funeral cortege through the town. It seemed like we drove for miles. Piet was a big deal in his home town and it seemed like everybody had turned out for his funeral. There were loads of roads closed. It wasn't an easy thing to do – I was in Tenerife when Piet died, so after we got home it was a rush to get everything together. We travelled overnight on Thursday, attended the funeral on Friday and came back on the ferry to race in the UK at the weekend. But it was something I wanted to do. Piet and I had spent many years racing with each other and he died doing what we both love to do.

Inevitably it was still a sombre atmosphere a year later when the World Cup came around again. The weather matched the occasion too – it was grey, dull and wet. They were conditions that suited me and I managed to take the win in the main event, with Dave Schaap and Stuart Smith Junior on the other steps of the podium.

After winning the main Dutch title for the third time, there followed eight years where I didn't lift the trophy. I was still there or thereabouts, with one second place and two third places during those years, but there's no doubt I fell behind the pace a little. First Ron Kroonder imposed himself as the top man in Dutch racing again, then Gary Castell started racing every weekend in the Netherlands and had plenty of money behind him to do it. That meant that, for a couple of years, he became the man to beat. Then the Brits invaded again, but it was two of the new generation, Tom Harris and Dan Johnson, who took the title.

This was the time when I was no longer the king on tarmac. I was struggling to find the time to dedicate to my own car, especially when Frankie and Phoebe started racing Ministox, and I was struggling to match the money that drivers like Gary Castell and Tom Harris were putting into their cars. It started to show in the grid positions I had in the World Cup race. The UK entrants were gridded by time trials during the afternoon. Obviously driver skill plays a role in getting a decent lap time, but if you had a car that was a few notches below what everybody else had, you couldn't do anything about it. That was the position I found myself in. In 2012 I qualified sixth-fastest among the Brits, beaten by Lee Fairhurst, Luke Davidson, Tom Harris, my brother Danny and Scott Davids. I recovered to fourth overall by the end but I was never going to win the race from the ninth row. In 2014 I was third-fastest, starting back on row six. Better, but still not ideal.

I had the same grid position in 2015, but there was a leveller – it was wet. I'd won before when it was wet, but this time I really needed it. Having a wet track is bound to remove some of the advantage that drivers in quicker cars have; drivers like Dan Johnson, Christiaan Weyenburg or Geert-Jan Keijzer, Piet's son. A wet track plays into the hands of older, more experienced drivers, and on the grid there was nobody older or more experienced than me!

A pile up on the first lap saw a restart but three of the Dutch drivers starting near me didn't make it out the second time, which gave me a bit of space when the green flag fell. I managed to manoeuvre my way through to third place by the third lap, taking advantage as other drivers struggled to handle the slick track. They were trying to hit too hard which meant that they followed the car they had hit onto the wetter outside line. I could just nip down the inside, the hard work done for me.

The same thing happened a couple of laps later. Geert-Jan Keijzer and Sjeng Smidt Junior had initially opened up a lead nearly the length of the straight but they kept knocking each other wide and crawling round the corners, allowing me to catch up quickly. When Geert tried it again, I just drove up the inside into second and, since I was on the line with better grip, got away from him down the home straight. Two laps later, after I'd closed the gap slightly to Sjeng, I knocked his back bumper. It wasn't hard enough for me to pass but it was hard enough to send him onto the wet. It put him a little out of sorts down the straight, so I knocked his back bumper again going into the next corner. He drifted onto the wet outside line again but I was still on the dry inside, so I got through for the lead.

That was the only time I needed to work to overtake, but it was nothing dramatic – just a couple of taps and I nipped through. I drove to the conditions and kept the lead until the chequered flag to take my third World Cup title, nine years after the second.

Being given the World Cup trophy was great, as always, but that paled into insignificance compared to a different gift I was given that year: a framed picture from Theo van Lier. On the back it said 'Thank you for saving my life'.

Theo was referring to the World Cup meeting a year earlier, when there was a big accident. After the World Cup race, which was won by Dan Johnson, there was a full race meeting. I won the first heat and got trackside to watch the second. The heat was restarted after Lee Robinson rolled early on and I wandered over to the pit gate to check whether Chris Cowley needed any help – he had broken his diff during the first lap. Soon after the restart, Tom Harris got behind Danny van Wamelen and gave him a massive push. Theo van Lier happened to be in front of Danny and took the brunt of the force, hitting the fence hard. Theo was knocked out and either his foot was on the throttle or it stuck, so he continued round the corner, past where I was stood, until he was hit by another couple of cars. Theo's car eventually came to rest a little down the straight and burst into flames.

There's no thinking at a moment like that. You just respond instinctively. I jumped over the fence and ran down the track while the cars were still moving. Luckily Rob Speak was one of the first cars round – he saw me running onto the track and stopped, blocking the way to protect me. I got to the side of the car while the fire was still raging and reached inside to undo Theo's belts. I knew that he needed to get out, but I couldn't lift him on my own.

The cab was filling with thick smoke so I put my hand over Theo's mouth to try to stop him breathing it in until more help came. Who knows how long it took – it was probably a couple of seconds but it seemed like hours. Then Chris Cowley, Ollie Ives, Dylan Williams-Maynard, Ben Hurdman and Dan Johnson got there to help. As the fire crew started to put the blaze out, we manhandled Theo out of the cab and let the medics and officials get to work.

I acted instinctively, on adrenaline, but when the initial burst of action was over, it got to me quite a bit. I was upset and angry. I genuinely thought that Theo was dead at that point. Tom got it off me, good and proper, but it was like he wasn't really there when I was giving him both barrels. I think he was in shock. The second time I spoke to him, we'd both calmed down. I told him that he needed to get loaded up and get out of there. The mood was beginning to turn a little ugly in the pits as people blamed him for the crash. You could see by then that he'd realised what he had done.

When you're a top driver, you know that you're going to get put in the fence – it's going to happen at some point. Usually, you know you'll give it back. I've put Tom in and he's put me in. That's life as a stock car driver. But when other drivers, particularly lower-grade drivers, end up as collateral damage for no real reason, that's just wrong. Theo had no idea that Tom was on a charge or was about to fence Danny van Wamelen, he was just having a race and minding his own business and nearly ended up dying. It was totally out of order.

Theo called me a hero afterwards, but you do what you have to do. He wasn't getting out on his own and I wasn't going to stand there and watch him burn to death. Maybe I was a bit dumb and put myself in harm's way, but I wasn't the only one to do so. I was just the quickest there. I don't have a bad turn of speed for an old man!

Theo suffered multiple fractures, damage from smoke inhalation and swelling of the brain but it could have been far worse. He was lucky that his fuel tank had split at the top of the back end. The fire came from fuel washing out of it. If the bottom of the tank had split, the fire would have been a huge inferno and nobody would have been able to do anything about it. For sure, the outcome would have been different.

After Theo was taken off to hospital and Tom had left, nobody knew what to do. The fans were still in the stadium but many of the drivers, especially the Dutch, didn't want to race. They thought they'd just witnessed one of their own being killed. I've been around a long time, so many of them gravitated towards me to ask what I thought. Some of the Dutch drivers were saying that they didn't want to race with any British driver because they thought we were too dangerous. I reassured them that we weren't there to cause problems. I went across to Theo's transporter and asked them what they wanted us to do. They thought that we should carry on racing.

I called the drivers together and explained that we should carry on racing. We should race for the fans in the stadium, many of whom had travelled a long way. We should race for the good of the drivers – I knew after Johnny Goodhall's crash that the best thing to do is get back in the car and get racing rather than dwelling on things. But most of all, we should race because it was the wish of Theo's team and family.

I fired up my car and drove it across to the pit gate. I was making a statement. Time to race. Thankfully, others began to follow my lead and, after a long gap, racing could finally continue. It was all a little tame and nobody took any risks, but it was still stock car racing.

On the eighteen occasions that the World Cup was run at Venray (or Warneton in 2008) up to and including 2016, I won three titles. That's a tally matched by Ron Kroonder and Henk-Jan Ronitz, which is pretty good company. But, alongside those wins, I've also finished second on three occasions and had four third-place finishes. Kroonder managed two of each, while Ronitz never stood on the podium except when he won. Still, I'll treasure that picture from Theo more than any of the other trophies.

Ouch!

17

I've pushed through the pack and there's only one more car to overtake, then I'll be in the lead. It shouldn't prove too much of a problem to get past Dean Whitwell – my car is visibly quicker down the long Hednesford straights.

I see Dean go wide round the corner at the end of the home straight so I take a tighter inside line. He stays wide down the back straight and I accelerate alongside him.

Three-quarters of the way down the back straight, we're so close that our wheels touch. Shit. There's hardly any contact, but it's enough to flick me into the air. I hold on for dear life as my car skids towards the infield on two wheels.

Then there's nothing. Just black.

Some crashes are the result of dangerous, aggressive or stupid driving but some are just bad luck. Lady luck finally caught up with me after twenty years, when I had the worst accident of my career at Hednesford. It was just a freak incident.

If I want to know what happened I have to watch the race on YouTube. I don't remember exactly. We charged down the straight with me on the inside and Dean on the outside. The straights are longer at Hednesford than any other British track we race at, so we were alongside each other for a few seconds. Then our tyres kiss. It wasn't my fault, it wasn't Dean's fault. It was just one of those things that happens when you're charging down a long straight and concentrating on the braking point.

Rollovers are one thing. You just hang on and wait for the ride to stop. My problem was that glancing wheels put me on my side and I hit the infield bank and its concrete Armco with the top of the roll cage. The momentum sent my car back out onto the track and I rolled over twice before coming to a halt on my roof.

The marshals were there pretty quickly – it was obviously a bad crash – and YouTube shows the first guy on the scene signalling with his hands as if to say it's all over. I was out cold. The impact with the banking broke the bottom seatbelt which made all the other belts go slack. During the crash I lifted out of the seat and hit my head on the roof of the car.

The crowd must have thought the worst when they put sheets up around the car to hide me from view. I'm sure some of the people who were right on the scene also thought the worst. The paramedics had a difficult decision to make. I wasn't breathing properly because my airway was blocked but they were also concerned that I'd suffered a spinal injury. They chose to flip the car back over, which was a gutsy call, but absolutely the right one. One of the paramedics spoke to me afterwards and said that she wasn't sure they'd made the right decision, but I told her that she was right. I was alive, wasn't I? She even had a bit of a ride herself – when they flipped the car back over she was trying to hang on to stabilise my neck, so she can now claim she's rolled over in a stock car too!

When the car went back on its wheels I sank back down into the seat and started breathing again. They cut the roof off the car and took me off the track in an ambulance, but not before I'd waved to the crowd to show them I was alright. I didn't get much of a ride in the ambulance because it stopped just off the track so the paramedics could have a good look over me and I told them I wanted to get out. My neck ached, but that was to be expected. I discharged myself and went back to the pits.

We did our best to get the car back into the transporter and I drove it back up to Silsden. Only after we'd parked up at home did I finally agree to go to Airedale Hospital with Sam. Once they heard what had happened to me, the hospital doctors crapped themselves and strapped me to a spinal board. I hated that, I completely freaked out – Sam says she has never seen me act like that before or since. I was swearing like a trooper, I'm ashamed of what I said to the nurses, but I just couldn't cope with being tied down like that. Eventually I kicked up such a fuss that they unstrapped me. I calmed down and apologised to the nurses. They were concerned that I'd do more damage but I told them that I'd had the accident ten hours ago and that I'd been walking and driving since. They couldn't understand my reasoning, but I really wasn't going back on the board.

After they looked at the x-rays, a doctor came in and delivered the news that I'd broken two vertebrae in my neck. It was stable so they put me in a collar and sent me home, there wasn't anything else they could do. Being the idiot I am, I took that as a green light to carry on with life as usual. I missed one weekend, just one race meeting, then I was back out on track at three meetings the following bank holiday weekend. The first race back I finished second to Mike Kingston (this time I decided not to overtake the yellow top for the lead!), the third meeting back I won the final at Belle Vue and came second in the Grand National from the lap handicap.

Brave or stupid? A bit of both, really. It didn't affect me mentally, but I did suffer physically afterwards, as you'd expect with a broken neck. But I had to win the Points title, which I did with a comfortable margin, and I also regained the silver roof in the Shootout after Andy Smith had won it the previous year. I also finished second in the British, second in the World Final and third in the European, so it was pretty close to being a great year, broken neck apart!

My neck has never been right ever since. Continually hitting walls in a car doesn't give it much chance to heal. I was lucky that I had a solid neck to start with. It's just pure muscle, especially down one side. After all, I've turned left all my life. When I first went to see a physio after the Hednesford crash, he couldn't understand what was going on with my neck – I don't have much movement in it. Eventually he worked out which bits are where and, when I go to see him every so often, he can help to loosen it off a bit. Considering how long I've been driving, that's the worst injury I've suffered in a stock car by far. I have a theory that the bodies of drivers who race from a young age adapt and learn to cope with the impact. That's the only way I can explain how I get put in the wall so hard and keep going.

I've driven in pain lots of times but often it isn't the result of stock cars – just my own clumsiness off the track. I drove with a broken arm in the World Semi-Final in 1992 after my road traffic accident, and I broke my foot a couple of years ago in the workshop. I dropped a back axle on my foot and heard something snap, so I knew I'd broken something. I went for an x-ray the next day and the doctor told me that I'd broken it, but it was a clean break and it had already started to heal. He said he'd never seen anything like it; the bone had calcified and begun to repair itself quicker than it should – I must be like Wolverine from X-Men!

I don't learn from my mistakes though. They put a plaster pot on to immobilise my foot and told me to take it easy. I had to use crutches to walk and I couldn't do anything. That's not me. I don't do doing nothing. I managed to last two days with the pot on, then I'd had enough. I cut it off with an angle grinder and went racing at the weekend.

I knew I'd have a bit of explaining to do when I went back to the fracture clinic about a month later. I was supposed to have been in a pot for four weeks, not two days, never mind racing a stock car. I didn't know how I was going to blag my way out of the fact that I hadn't been wearing it. I was supposed to get the pot cut off before I saw a doctor. I was in the waiting room and a nurse walked towards me, looked surprised and said 'oh, they've already cut it off – that was quick, I was about to do it myself.' I tried to look straight-faced and innocent – that's quite hard to do – and said 'yes, yes, they've just done it.' The doctor looked at the x-rays and told me that it had healed perfectly! He told me to check that I didn't have any pain when I moved it, but he didn't know I'd been walking around on it for a month.

Although I wouldn't advise people to do the same, I think Sam was glad I ground it off – she said I was hell to live with for the two days that I did have the pot on; I stomped around like a bear with a sore head. She's probably right – I belong behind the wheel, not sat on the sofa!

Somewhere in the tyre smoke I'm celebrating
winning the UK Open!

18

The UK Open Championship can be a tricky one to win. It's the start of the year, the silly season in the grading list. Some drivers have won races from white and yellow and suddenly end up at the back of the grid with the stars and superstars, while other drivers are undergraded and start closer to the front than they should.

Not that I'll ever be undergraded. I've been a superstar for over twenty years. I've started at the back as usual, although I did manage to sneak past a lot of cars in the crush on the first couple of laps. Now I'm chasing down the rest, smiling to myself as I see Andy Smith parked up against the fence.

As the race comes to a close, I'm chasing down the lower graders who got away at the start. First up is Steve Hopkins, then Dean Whitwell. The last car I need to pass is a white-top who has made his debut this weekend and looks quick straight away. Lee Fairhurst is his name. He'll probably be one to watch in the future.

Anyway, this weekend is all about me. I move Fairhurst aside with three laps to go and get away to the chequered flag, although credit to Lee, he doesn't give up without a fight.

I've won the first championship of 2009, in front of BBC television cameras as well. I'm going to be a TV star!

At the end of 2007, the stock car world shifted slightly for me. My dad announced that he was retiring. It was no surprise, really. He was sixty years old and had been sliding down the grading list for a while. Although he was still competitive with a blue roof, in 2005 he hadn't won a single race. However, he was still a popular driver and fans flocked from all over to see him on his season-long farewell tour, and so they should too. He raced for thirty-eight years, during which he won the World and European titles and the National Points Championship three times. He is still equal-fourth on the list of final winners (tied with Willie Harrison, which seems apt since they both had long careers). For a while he was the number one challenger to Stuart Smith, which I'm sure helped gain him a lot of fans.

Dad purposely picked his final meeting to be at Sheffield in November because it came a few days after my little brother Danny's sixteenth birthday. He wanted his final meeting, which was branded the Frankie Wainman Testimonial, to be Danny's first ever F1 meeting. Danny even finished tenth in the meeting final, beating both me and my dad, although we beat him in the three-car Wainman match race. My dad won that. I let him, of course, since it was his testimonial. Although I would say that, wouldn't I?

It was going to be fun racing with Danny. There would be times over the next few years that I would appreciate having a friendly face out on track and I hoped that he could help tip the balance in a family-based battle that was developing in the sport. Towards the end of the 2000s, there were only two names in Formula 1 stock cars worth bothering about: Wainman and Smith. In 2007, the last time the British Championship had been won by somebody other than me or Andy Smith was 1998. The National Points Championship went back even further, to 1993. And, after I won the World Final in 2005, Andy Smith took the title in 2006.

Inevitably, there was a big rivalry developing. We shared two of the big titles between us again in 2007. I won back the silver roof after losing it to Andy for the first time in ages the year before, winning the National Series and finishing on top the grading points chart for good measure. Andy was second. He won the British Championship, I was second. When it came to the World Final, a new driver got onto the top step, breaking our domination. But it was still a bloody Smith!

I started that World Final at King's Lynn on the outside of the front row, and no surprise that Andy Smith was the guy on pole. The first half of the race was a real spectacle – Andy started off in the lead but I got past him after three laps, then he took the lead again, then Mark Gilbank took over, then Andy got back in front once again. Stuart Smith Junior was in the running too and I saw a chance to get rid of them both on the seventh lap. I was running in third at that point but I tried to take the lead by hitting Stuart into Andy and getting round them both. It didn't quite work, but it did succeed in dropping Andy so far down the places that he was effectively out of the race.

While the three of us scrapped it out, Mat Newson took the lead – the sixth change of lead in the first seven laps. Then we started to spread out a little bit. I knew that my car would come good at the end of the race so I didn't worry too much when Mat and Stuart started to pull away, although Lee Robinson did delay me a bit. I was close enough to sneak through the inside of Mat for second place at the same time that Stuart got past him, leaving the two of us in a five-lap blast for the World title.

The gap slowly narrowed until I was close enough for a last-bender. It was now or never. I hit Stuart hard and he pushed against a lap-down Dutch car, but he managed to keep going and squeezed over the line less than a second in front of me. I've finished second in plenty of World Finals – at the last count, I've been the first loser on seven occasions, way more than anybody else – but the 2007 World Final was the closest finish I had ever had. The margin of victory was so tight.

So now there was another Smith to battle. In 2008 we shared the major titles again – this time Andy won the World Final, Stuart won the British Championship and I retained the National Series silver roof and topped the grading points.

Andy Smith and I had been competing since Ministox days and there were plenty of times that we'd clashed on the track. The 1995 National Points Championship was probably where it all began, but it carried on through the next decade and beyond. Sometimes it crept off the track too, like when Andy challenged my World Final win in 1998 or when the rules were changed to take the silver roof away from the driver who won the most points over the season. When both of us were challenging for major honours and sharing the championships between us, it was difficult not to make it personal. I knew that whenever I went out on track, the person who stood most chance of stopping me was Andy. I'm sure that he thought exactly the same thing. There was added bite because his dad and my dad had been rivals during their career too, and Stuart Senior wasn't shy when it came to championing his son over me.

It was real Wars of the Roses stuff – two families battling for success, the rivalry passed down from fathers to sons, with the two sides based in Yorkshire and Lancashire too. It was such a great story that it came to the attention of a filmmaker called John Lakey, who came to us and said that he wanted to do a promotional video at a meeting to see if he could drum up interest in a documentary series. I helped him set it up and he turned up at the track to film his footage, but it absolutely chucked it down with rain. It wasn't ideal conditions to showcase our sport and I didn't think much would come from it.

John edited the footage and took it to the BBC. The executive he pitched to was a woman and I'm not sure that John was confident that she would be interested – after all, it was a film about boys playing with their toys in the mud and rain! They sat down together and John said she turned to him and said that she really liked it. He couldn't believe how positive her reaction was.

The following season John turned up with a film crew and backing for a six-part documentary series called *Gears and Tears* to be shown on BBC One. We were told that the central story was going to be the rivalry between the Wainmans and the Smiths – fair enough, that was the biggest thing going on in the sport at the time – with side stories developed for some of the other drivers. Rob and Chris Cowley got some airtime – who can forget Rob revealing his backside to the nation – with Paul Hines, who is a great ambassador for our sport. They focused on the personalities rather than the racing, but that's what they always wanted and that's what we knew they were going to do.

Possibly it's a good thing they didn't concentrate too much on the racing because it was definitely a year when the Smiths managed to get one up on me. They shared the big three titles between themselves – Stuart won the British Championship and the first ever National Points Shootout for the silver roof while Andy won the World Final. I was on top of the grading points table, but of course that didn't mean any silverware, and I finished second in the World Final. It was the first time since 1995 I hadn't won the British Championship or silver or gold roof.

It was amazing how much work went into creating six thirty-minute programmes. I think they ended up with over 2,000 hours of footage. Capturing the racing was probably the easy part – they knew where and when they needed to be and roughly what was going to happen – but they also travelled all over the place to film us. Given the amount of time they spent with us and knowing that they also had to film with the Smiths, Cowleys, Neachells, Paul Hines and Paul Harrison, who knows how many man-hours they spent on it. The crew were a nice gang but sometimes we'd have to go out of our way for them, to be at home when we had places we needed to be, or to meet them elsewhere.

The cameras wanted to capture everything, although there were certain things I didn't want them to film. When I had problems with my engine the day before the European Championship, the film crew came along with me to Ian Whitworth's to watch us work on it. Ian is a long-standing friend of mine and he has worked on my engines since the mid-nineties. I'll go over there and help him out. I strip and clean the engines them – the easy bit – and he assembles them. I'll often clean other bits for other engines while he is doing mine. Over the years we've bodged some of my engines back together, mainly because I haven't been able to afford top-line replacements. The trouble this time was that the cam had broken but we could not get it out. We tried all sorts of things but it wouldn't budge.

Eventually, I decided it needed radical action. I decided to weld a bolt to the cam follower so I could pull it out with brute force. It wasn't pretty but it was the only way I was going to race the next day. I wasn't keen being filmed doing that, and Ian knew what I was going to do and didn't want to watch, so I sent Ian down to the sandwich shop with the *Gears and Tears* crew. When they came back, the cam had miraculously come out!

Another thing I wasn't sure about them filming was when Frankie did his first testing session in his Ministox at Buxton. When I told the *Gears and Tears* team what we were going to do, they said that they'd love to film it, but I wasn't keen. I didn't want Frankie to be put under extra pressure, to feel like he had to perform for the cameras. His first drive on an oval racetrack would only ever happen once and I wanted it to be a father-son thing. I took Frankie to one side and asked him what he thought. He said that he didn't mind the cameras being there – he just thought it would be a bit of fun. I chatted to Beth, one of the crew, and told her that they could film but I wanted them to stand back a bit. She told me that wouldn't work – if they were filming, they needed to be able to get our faces. Otherwise it would be a waste of time.

In the end I gave in. They filmed it properly and got what they wanted and it ended up being a good scene in the programme – even if he did manage to crash on an empty track! The producers put a film together of all the footage of Frankie driving that day, about thirty minutes in all, and I'm really glad we've got that now.

Frankie came across as a cute little kid, so did Phoebe. I'm probably not the best person to judge how I came across myself, but I think I did alright. It was clear that Andy and I weren't the best of friends but I think it showed our competitive sides. The wives weren't so lucky. Lisa Smith and Samantha probably came out of the programme worst. The cameras captured all of their bickering and bitching and made Sam and Lisa out to be the bad guys. Let's face it, they can both be gobby cows – you're never going to stop that! But it also showed how much stock car racing meant to both of them. Both Sam and Lisa are 100% supportive of their husbands, and you can't fault them for that. What you didn't see was a lot of the good stuff they were saying. The editing emphasised the arguments and chopped out the nice comments, and the rivalry was a bit hyped up by the crew who encouraged them to say things about each other. It has certainly made us more forgiving when we watch somebody looking like an idiot on *Wife Swap* or *Come Dine With Me* – now we wonder whether it's all in the editing!

Even so, I'm glad we were involved. Yes, it was time consuming, intrusive and surprisingly hard work, but the way it lifted the profile of the sport was amazing. The following year, when the programme had aired, the World Final was a sell out at Coventry. It brought a lot of people back to the sport who had moved on after their local stadium had closed – Odsal, Aycliffe, Long Eaton and the like. It still has an impact today. I was stood in the queue at KFC in a motorway services the other day and this big bodybuilder guy tapped me on the shoulder. I turned around and thought uh-oh, what does this man-mountain want? He said, 'You're that guy from the stock cars, aren't you? I watched you on TV. It was brilliant. We watched every one!' And that was seven years after it was shown. He'd never been to a meeting, never probably will, but *Gears and Tears* made people aware of the sport.

I think I'll have to get an agent and audition for more television work. I reckon I'd make a great Doctor Who!

After winning a record third 240 Championship
on the other side of the world

19

Stock car racing is an individual sport. I compete on my own against thirty-odd other rivals on the track. There can only be one winner and my plan is to make sure that it's me.

So it's an odd feeling to be rolling out on track in a car plastered with the Union Jack and wearing blue and red overalls with Great Britain written on them. When the green flag falls, it's my job to complete my laps and cross the finish line first. No change there. But there are only eight cars on track, two of which have no intention of doing anything other than taking me out. Luckily I have two drivers on my side who aren't interested in winning the race – they just want to protect me and take out the opposition.

Welcome to the first ever race of the British Lions in the slightly surreal and often explosive world of team racing.

New Zealand has become my second home. I reckon I've raced on the other side of the world twenty times now and I have no intention of stopping. What's more, I've done pretty well out there. In the World 240 Championship – the Kiwi equivalent of our World Final – I've been the top foreign finisher on fifteen occasions.

Such was my love of New Zealand racing that I decided to build my own superstock in Silsden and ship it across to the other side of the world to race there. For years I'd been relying on people like Stan and Sonja Hickey to find me cars and look after them and they'd done a great job, but now I fancied a bit more independence. I certainly hadn't fallen out with anybody – the Hickeys still housed the car for me and remain good friends to this day – nor was it because I thought I could do a better job than the Kiwi builders. It was just something I wanted to do for my own enjoyment. I had a bit of spare cash, so why not?

I travelled home from New Zealand in 2005 in a party of four and I don't think we had a spare set of underwear between us! We left all our gear in New Zealand so I could transport home a fibreglass superstock body and all the components that I couldn't get in the UK. I cut the body up into pieces and we used that for our luggage allowance. Luckily that year we travelled via the USA and for some reason we all had sixty-four kilograms each, so all in all we came back with just short of a quarter of a tonne of stock car parts. I needed to check it all in as oversized baggage, the person behind the counter there must have thought we were nutters!

Once it was safely back in Silsden, I set to work putting it all back together. Over the next nine months or so it slowly started to look like a superstock again. The car was how I wanted it to be – the roll cage was a bit more secure than the typical New Zealand ones because I wasn't keen on some of the big gaps that they have across there. Take off the fibreglass body and there's very little protection in some of them. I also put together a Volvo transporter truck to take it from meeting to meeting. Both car and lorry had to go back to the other side of the world and I sent a load of gearboxes in the truck too to sell when I got across there to help finance the shipping. The bill was nearly ten grand, so it wasn't something I was doing to make a profit, it was a labour of love. It all started a slow seven-week voyage by ship; I flew across to meet it when it arrived.

Both the car and I arrived a few days before Christmas and I couldn't wait to pick it up. Then I received news that the shipment was stuck in the docks and wasn't going to be unloaded for two weeks. My stuff was in the wrong part of the ship and they were unloading another bit first, then the dock workers were clocking off for Christmas and wouldn't be back until 3 January. I was crestfallen. I'd spent a year getting the car and truck ready, only to miss most of the race meetings I was there for.

A few people told me that they'd sort a car for me to race, but I wanted my own. I drove up to the docks with Danny, who was fourteen at the time, to see if there was anything I could do. I blagged my way into the docks and ended up in the canteen where all the workers eat. One of them started chatting to me and it turned out that he was the spare, on-call crane driver. All he had to do was sit around watching telly until he was called upon. I told him that I'd shipped a racing car across from the UK and was seeing if I could get it out before Christmas. Luckily he showed an interest. He'd heard about superstock racing and had vaguely heard of me, although he wasn't a stock car racing fan. He told me that he was going to have a word with his boss to see what he could do.

A few minutes later he came back and told me that his boss had given permission to unload the truck and car with a forklift, but that if there was any damage or anything went wrong, they couldn't be held responsible. The on-call crane driver was willing to give it a go, so I said that we should take the risk and go for it.

When he first mentioned using a forklift to lift the truck, I thought the plan sounded a bit odd. But when he turned up, it suddenly made sense. This forklift truck was massive! The Volvo lorry was on a flat rack because it was too big for a standard container, but the forklift got it out no problem and carefully dropped it to the dockside.

The next problem was that the truck was stuck on the flat rack. It's a big, flat, metal palette with two metal sides, but they fold inwards, not out, so you couldn't just drive the truck off. It also needed to be lifted with a crane. The crane driver looked at it and said, 'I reckon I can lift the truck with the forklift – but you're going to have to go under the chassis and block it off to help.' So he lifted it and Danny and I were putting blocks of wood under. It had to go about ten feet in the air to clear the flat rack and it was one of the scariest things I've ever seen. The truck was painted up and looked pristine, and I'd spent months working on the superstock inside. I had visions of the whole thing falling to the concrete and being a write-off. When the wheels finally touched the ground, I breathed a huge sigh of relief.

After that, we had to take the truck to the customs post. It was spotless, the whole thing had been sandblasted and painted before it was sent across, but they still insisted that we unload everything; the car, all the parts, all the gearboxes, so they could be cleaned in case there were any environmental contaminants. Danny and I spent hours unloading and loading everything. Eventually we got the all clear, my boxes were ticked and we set off. I felt as proud as anything; it was one of the best moments of my stock car life. I was on top of the world.

That feeling lasted for about 200 metres. We pulled up at the main gate and a woman stopped the truck, looked through the window, stared at Danny and said, 'How old is he?' I told her – fourteen – and she said, 'Wait here.'

I never did catch her name, so I'll call her the Ayatollah's wife. She stomped off and came back with a couple of official-looking men and berated me for bringing an underage child onto the docks. She properly kicked off. I told her that nobody had said anything when we first arrived, that we'd seen plenty of people while we were there and nobody had said anything, and that she was the first person to pick up on it – about ten hours after we had arrived. We hadn't lied about it, nobody had asked. They argued amongst themselves for a while and eventually I got them to let us out. After all, it was their problem, not mine.

So I drove away from the docks feeling as proud as anything; it was one of the best moments of my stock car life. I was on top of the world. Again.

Danny and I travelled down to Rotorua where there was a race meeting. Nobody was expecting us to turn up with the car – they all thought I would have spent the day arguing with the dock workers and would come back with my tail between my legs. They thought they wouldn't see the car until the season later. Although it was too late to compete, I drove into the pits with the truck and unloaded the car so everybody could see it. It was mint.

That year's trip was one of the best I've had. We were on the road for two weeks on the South Island, racing every day or every other day. There were probably fourteen of us drivers travelling around together with our crews, staying on the same campsites and enjoying ourselves. I was already well known in New Zealand after racing there for a decade, but now that I was racing with my own car and own truck, it made people even more welcoming. I think that people appreciated the commitment I'd shown to superstock racing and I noticed a real turnaround in many people's opinions of me. I gained a whole lot of respect, on and off the track. I think that still remains today.

The new car went well. There inevitably a few teething problems with the power steering and such like, so the first time out I came seventh in the World 240s. I had everything sorted for the next year, 2007, where I got another third place. Then the following year I was fourth, losing a run-off for third place with Roydon Collingwood after finishing level with him on points.

In 2009, I drew grid nineteen for the first race, the inside of the tenth row. The grids change around each time so a driver starts one heat towards the front, one in the middle and one towards the back, so I knew that the first race would be my worst grid position of the evening. My plan was to give it a go and hope for the best and I was really pleased when I ended the race in fifth place. What's more, it was already clear that I was going to be the only Brit with a chance of winning. Tom Harris had started on the fourth row but dropped back to twentieth, Stuart Smith Junior started to my outside but came home one place behind Tom, and Mark Taylor didn't finish at all – a death sentence as far as his championship hopes were concerned.

What I needed now was a bit of support from the Brits. We British drivers don't go into the World 240s with the mindset that one of our drivers should win. We're too used to racing individually and it's hard to get out of that mindset. But this time I was clearly the only one with a chance and, with a bit of help, I got third place in the second heat.

Going into the final race, I was top of the standings. I was the obvious target for Kiwi drivers to take out, never mind that I was a pom. Palmerston drivers are always strong and there were four different Palmy drivers within a few points of me: Roydon Collingwood, Shane Penn, Andy McCabe and Peter Bengston. Christchurch's Malcolm Ngatai was also close, as was Rotorua's Pat Westbury, but he would be expected to support Stan Hickey, who was second in the points. The Kiwi drivers who had no chance would now be looking for the top-scoring drivers from other tracks and going out with no intention other than to stop them. The Brits aren't really good at that; I knew I couldn't rely on Stuart, Tom and Mark deliberately stopping another driver who might win a championship just so I could win – it's just too alien to them. But I knew I had an advantage in the points and I hoped it would be enough.

I started fifteenth, right in the middle of the pack. As always, the last race of the 240 Championship was a slog. I had Kiwi drivers trying to take me out and Brits putting the bumper in to support me. Roydon Collingwood started on the front row but I could see that he was out of the running. Stan Hickey started near the back and when the race was stopped at one point, I had a look around and could see that he wasn't a threat. Then I had a look around to see where the other Brits are, to see if they could lend me a hand.

When the race got going again, it just went ballistic. I just had to hold on, keep my foot down and keep away from the wall. Tom and Mark were just behind and trying to keep an eye on me, but at one stage Tom tried to block for me and ended up giving me a big hit! I had to get going again because you can't be stationary in superstocks, you're just a sitting duck if that happens. I didn't make as much progress as I hoped. I hobbled over the line in ninth place with both inside tyres flat and had to fend off another attack – the racing doesn't stop until the red flag comes out. There was no way I wasn't going to finish, even if I had to crawl around, but finishing in the middle of the pack meant that I was dependent on other results to challenge for the title.

I sat in the car trying to work out my own points and those of my rivals, but it's not easy with so many to consider. One difference in superstock racing is that you don't get lap boards or your position indicated during the race, so trying to work out which driver is in which position is really difficult. I was confident of a podium, but I didn't know where. Once the points were totted up, it showed that I'd won by a solitary point. Pat Westbury had come second in the race which gave him second overall – had he managed to win, he'd have tied with me. It was a similar situation for Malcolm Ngatai – he finished the last heat in third and came third overall, but a win in that last race would have brought him level with me too. So I was very pleased that Scott Miers took the chequered flag. Whether his countrymen thought the same, I'm not so sure!

The same year I won my third 240 title was also the same year that, for the first time, I was able to take part in another great New Zealand event: the Superstock Team Championship. It's a unique set of races that doesn't have an equivalent in Britain or the Netherlands. Because each driver is affiliated to a track, once a year each track puts forward a team of drivers to compete against the others. Points are gained for the positions that each driver finishes in, but this isn't a simple race where everybody is shooting for the chequered flag. Instead it's a tactical battle. Each team will have runners, who try to finish the race, but also blockers, whose job is to stop the other team's runners. The result is often carnage!

I'd watched plenty of team races since I'd first raced in New Zealand and I always wanted to get involved, but I didn't think it would happen. Setting up a British team to compete on the other side of the world, when most British drivers had never raced as a team and most had never even raced in a superstock? It sounded like a fantasy. Things changed around 2007 when I had a chat with Guy Parker. He had been around the stock car scene for a while and was one of my mechanics for a period, coming along to New Zealand on one of my trips. That really got him into New Zealand stock cars and eventually he started to look more seriously into taking a bunch of British drivers to the other side of the world to compete. He asked me if I thought we could make it work. I told him probably not!

Then Stuart Smith Junior, who raced in New Zealand in 2008, also got wind of the idea and asked me whether it would be possible to put a British team together. We both decided to give it a go if some other drivers could be found. All credit to Guy, he put in huge amounts of work finding other team members, liaising with the organisers and finding some cars for us to use to make the whole thing a reality. It was a huge task. As a result of his work, the British Lions rolled out on track for the first time in 2009: Stuart and I were joined by Mark Taylor with Tom and Mick Harris.

I decided to use my own superstock that I'd built at home and shipped across the world. That was a risky thing to do – there's plenty of damage in Team Championship races – but in that first year we were scrabbling around for cars and it seemed wrong that I had a good car that was going to sit unused.

Given my experience at the World 240s, I thought that the Brits would be cannon fodder, the team that every-body would want to beat because they would hate for a foreign team to win. Actually, it was the opposite. We got instant support. Whoever we were against, all the other team supporters cheered for us and we became everybody's second-favourite team.

It probably helped that our first race saw us put in a really gutsy performance against the Palmerston North Panthers. They were the defending champions, full of top Kiwi names; we were the underdogs, but we got fantastic support from the crowd. And we really shook the Kiwis up! We didn't win the tie but we showed everybody that we weren't going to be an easy rollover and we were there to compete. The next race was against the Manawatu Mustangs and this time we were superb, we raced them off the park and I got the win for the team.

Each team tends to have two runners, whose job is to go for the race win, and two blockers, who are there to stop the opposition runners. I started off as one of the runners because it's what I've had to do as long as I've raced in New Zealand – get to the finish line and avoid Kiwis who are trying to take me out. Blocking is a different skill entirely. New Zealand drivers are used to it, but it's a strange skill to us.

The loss against Palmerston meant that the best we could achieve on the second evening was third place. We set ourselves up for the podium with a 1-2-3 finish against the Hawkes Bay Hawkeyes, then Stuart crossed the line first against the Stratford Scrappers. To finish our first ever Team Championship in third place was a superb achievement. Everybody contributed, everyone did their job. I was well known over there after so many appearances in the World 240s and Stuart had taken to superstock racing well the year before, but the driver who really made an impact was Tom Harris. He was able to hit and block really well considering that he had never raced in a team event and had never raced in a superstock. It was the first year they'd ever seen Tom in New Zealand and he made quite an impression.

Having the British Lions in the Team Championship was a great spectacle. It rejuvenated the event: it increased the credibility of the championship and brought the crowd through the turnstiles; it was a sell-out both nights.

Obviously we took some damage in the cars that we loaned, but we repaired or paid for everything so they were given back in the same condition that they were given to us. Nobody went out and trashed a car unnecessarily. It meant that we were able to find cars again for the next year, and the year after that. Since 2009, I've raced in every Team GB campaign but one. After the good start in 2009, we improved to second place in 2010. Then results turned very average for a few years: fifth in 2011, third in 2012, sixth in 2013 and 2014 (the year that I missed) and eighth in 2015. But things have perked up again, with second place in both 2016 and 2017.

Some top UK drivers have taken part for the British Lions: Tom Harris, Mat Newson, Stuart Smith Junior, Craig Finnikin, Lee Fairhurst, my brother Danny. But it isn't necessarily the superstars who convert to team racing the best. I've raced alongside a major championship winner from the UK who struggled mentally to cope in a team race and I needed to constantly gee him up.

We need five drivers who each understand what the other is doing and who get the idea of team racing. They've got to do the role that they are given, whatever it is. If they don't play their part, the others can't do theirs. They don't need to be the best UK driver, they don't have to be the fastest UK driver, they just need to complete the task they are given. I need to be able to rely on the other three British cars when I'm out on track, just as they should know that I would put myself on the line for them. It's more about the character of the driver than it is their driving skill. Mick Harris is a good example. He did exactly what we told him to do: no big hits, he just slowed people down like we needed him to. If they're bright and intelligent and don't put themselves in a position to get hurt, they won't get hurt.

We try to coach the lads the best we can. In recent years, I've tried to step back from any warm-up races and let the younger, less experienced drivers have a go. I've been there and done it on many occasions so a 'friendly' against one of the track teams isn't that much use to me, but it can be invaluable to one of the new drivers. They all say their thing beforehand, saying that they can take it and they'll give out some big hits, but when push comes to shove, some of them just don't like it. They freeze. Other people thrive on it. I can tell after the first race whether they will take to it. What do they look like when they get out of the car? Chris Cowley was buzzing after his first go. He said, 'That hurt – but I loved it!' Once he said that, I knew he'd be fine. He enjoyed it, so he did his job properly.

It also helps me to learn a little more about the other British drivers. We all go out together and have dinner beforehand. It helps us to bond as a team and get to know each other. The New Zealand track teams race together week in, week out and know each other inside out. Sometimes, we don't. Recently, Michael Scriven was part of the team. I'd never really had much to do with him before, but we got chatting over a few dinners and found out a little more about each other. I realised that I could rely on him and, by the time the Team Championship races were over, we'd formed a really solid bond.

So we've finished as runners-up three times now in the Team Championship and we've grown into real competitors. I'm used to finishing second in major competitions, but part of me was pleased when I saw how badly Lee Fairhurst and Ben Hurdman took it when we lost those finals. It showed me how much they want to win. Having drivers like that make the team stronger. Lee is turning into a good runner too, which means that it doesn't have to fall on me. We can switch things around and try to confuse the opposition. I've done a bit of blocking and had a few of the Kiwis over the wall and I really enjoyed doing that. It felt like giving them a taste of their own medicine!

The respect and thanks we get for putting in the effort of going over there is great. You don't get it anywhere else. Get in front of the grandstand, pull up in your cars there, and it's mental. When we win it – and we will, one year – it will be a great ovation.

Racing under the Union Jack is great, but I've also continued to race for myself in the World 240 Championship. Since my last title win I've had another four trophies for the top foreigner, including second place in 2014 to Peter Bengston. I was three points behind Peter in the end, and that's a massive gap in the 240 Championship, so he was a worthy winner. Anyway, although I wasn't on the top step, that second place meant that I'd now stood on the 240 podium seven times. Considering that the next best total is four, I'm pretty happy. And, of course, I've won the title three times – more than any other, including the Kiwis.

Frankie keeps a close eye as I spray
his roof gold for the first time

20

Wainman is on pole position in the gold-top race. Only this time, it's not me. I'm watching.

Young Frankie has been outstanding in his Ministox this season, especially at Barford, which is hosting the Ministox National Championship to decide the winner of the gold roof. But it's easy to forget that Frankie JJ is still only twelve years old and racing against some really canny fifteen year olds. I told him to expect a rough ride!

I strap him in and give him a hug. Now it's down to him. I've never felt so helpless and nervous before a race. Frankie seems relaxed and chilled.

We chatted about the race in the build up and I explained that the starts will be the key. I watch as Frankie takes complete control of the rolling lap and floors the accelerator and just the right moment. He takes off down the home straight and pulls enough of a gap to avoid being hit on the first corner.

Although he has a good lead, the race is stopped by waved yellows. Now he has to do it all again. And again, he holds the grid until the green flag drops and makes a textbook getaway. Then the race stops again. I'm not sure my nerves can handle this. But Frankie does another perfect couple of corners and gets away cleanly again.

He holds on until the chequered flag to claim the Ministox gold roof. I sprint to the finish line as Frankie takes of his helmet. I'll never forget the smile on his face. He turns to me and, cool as a cucumber, says 'Was that okay, Dad?'

Okay? Are you for real? It was better than okay, it was perfect!

At the start of the first episode of *Gears and Tears*, my dad was interviewed while driving the transporter to a meeting. He said that I'd mellowed, that I wasn't as hard as a used to be, that I'd lost confidence, and blamed it on my accident at Hednesford in 2007. I don't agree. I was still confident in my ability and I don't think the crash at Hednesford, bad as it was, changed my driving. I've always been insanely competitive and I think I always will. It doesn't matter what I'm doing or where I am, I have to win. If the family and I go anywhere like ten-pin bowling, which we often do on New Years' Eve, I always have to win!

However, it's true that my form began to drop off a little bit and that it coincided with *Gears and Tears*. For five years from 2009, I didn't win one of the four major championships and was left picking up smaller titles like the UK Open, Grand National Championship and World of Shale. It was still silverware, but not what I was used to. You can probably sum up why I stopped winning big titles in one word: Ministox. When the kids reached the age where they could start racing, my own results began to tail off a little. I was still there or thereabouts – I finished with the second-highest number of points in 2010, 2011 and 2012 – but I no longer dominated like I used to. But it was a choice I made, and one I don't regret at all. Phoebe and Frankie's racing careers were just beginning and I felt that my first responsibility as a parent was to help them race. How any driver starts their career is very important. If the people around them are supportive and enthusiastic, it's likely they will enjoy it. If they felt that their racing was just a second thought, they might lose interest and drift away.

I had a crap deal in Ministox. My dad was in a different situation – he was building up a new business and couldn't give me the time that I needed to make it a success. But because I knew that I'd struggled in Minis, I didn't want my kids to too. They cost a lot of money for sure, and I can see now why my dad couldn't afford it, but I did what I could. I sold my New Zealand superstock after running it for six or so years to help pay for the kids' Ministox. Although the superstock served me well, if it was going to carry on being competitive it really needed a new engine. I built it with a small-block Chevy, similar to what we run in the UK, but superstocks began to move towards Nissan and Toyota quad cams and it couldn't compete engine-wise. Although that car was a labour of love, I could either spend a wad of cash upgrading it or I could offload it and put the money towards Frankie and Phoebe. It was an easy choice to make. I think the superstock is still out there on track now, still with the same Chevy in it, now racing under a new owner.

I needed to get building again, but it was a long time since I had raced a Ministox and they'd changed a lot since the mid-1980s. Now the cars are all custom-built with a space-frame chassis. I needed to learn how to build and maintain them. Although there were some similarities with a Formula 1 stock car, there were lots of differences. I was lucky to find a whole load of parts when I bought a stock car and engine from Chris Elwell just as Frankie was starting out. When I pulled up at his yard, I saw an old Ministox on top of a container. I recognised it from years back and, after I asked Chris about it, it turned out that his son had raced Ministox and then suddenly decided that he didn't want to race anymore. It had been sat there ever since – probably around 2002, seven years before I turned up at the yard. I did a deal to take away two old Ministox and loads of spare parts, and those parts were vital to me learning the trade. While I learned the ropes on Ministox and continued the bread-and-butter business of building and repairing stock cars for other drivers, my own stock cars ended up being the last priority.

Frankie was the first to start racing in the final few meetings of 2009, in a car that we'd been working on all season. Phoebe soon followed on. Although she was older, she wasn't bothered about racing at first. Like Frankie, I'd borrowed somebody else's car and taken her for a practice at Buxton when she was ten. She was really good but basically left the track saying thanks but no thanks. Although

I wanted her to race and knew that she could do well, I knew that she had to make the decision. You can't make a kid do it. After Frankie started, we went the end-of-season awards dinner and he got presented with an award for the youngest driver or something. Throughout the night, I could see Phoebe chatting with all the girls who raced and were her age like Holly Gould and Terri-Ann Smith. I whispered to Sam, 'You listen to Phoebe on the way home.' We got in the car and lo and behold: 'Dad, is it alright if I race in a meeting?' My answer? 'I'd love you to!'

I found an old car that Danny used to race and she made her debut in that at a Christmas meeting at Skegness. The weather was horrible. It was absolutely freezing, but Phoebe did really well and enjoyed it. I knew that if she was happy to race in those conditions, she'd be hooked for life! I refurbished one of the old Elwell cars for her and she never looked back. Now she loves it. Ever since, she complains that I didn't force her to race when she was younger, but it doesn't work like that, it has to be a child's own decision. It would have pushed her away. But that doesn't matter to Phoebe – she says she's going to strap her own kid in a car and make them go out to race!

When Phoebe's short time in Ministox came to an end, she chose to carry on driving in V8 Hotstox. It made a lot of sense. She knew that F1 wasn't the right place for a sixteen-year-old girl. Now she absolutely loves it. It's been a great formula for her and I think she's been good for the formula – like it or not, the Wainman name brings with it a certain amount of attention and, although I sometimes wish the kids didn't have so many eyes on them, it's really helped to lift the profile of the V8s.

Both Frankie and Phoebe were natural drivers. For me, that was awesome. If you nurture a natural driver, they'll get better and better. They just get in a car and get on with it. John Lund is a natural driver, it's just in him. Of course, there are good drivers who aren't natural drivers. Some drivers – Bobby Burns would be one – had to work at it. I'm sure he used the bumper a lot to make up for the a lack of natural skill, which is fine, it's stock car racing after all. But Frankie and Phoebe are definitely more on Lundy's end of the scale.

When I saw them doing well and having fun doing it, it made everything worthwhile. Frankie's gold roof races were fantastic. One of the best moments of my life was when Frankie won his first National Championship at Barford. He was tiny! He shouldn't have won that, kids don't win the gold top at twelve years old, but he won it proper. He went out there to win it. Phoebe got third place the year before in 2011, her only gold top race, in a new car I had built for her by Mark Webster. If she'd had a few more years, I'm sure she'd have picked up more po-diums too. Then Frankie won his second National Championship in 2014, getting over the line a metre or so ahead of Jedd Stirk in probably the best finish ever to a Ministox National Championship race. That my niece Camey Dorrell was in third made that victory even sweeter. Although I was a bit miffed that Frankie managed to pick up two gold roofs in his first five years of racing – didn't he know that it took his old man took twenty-two years to do that?

Anyway, it quickly became obvious that while the kids were picking up race wins and having a great time doing it, my own F1 racing was taking a back seat. However, I'm confident I'd have picked up the silver roof if they hadn't changed the rules again. Presumably the National Series hadn't done what they wanted it to, because I still won the silver roof in seven years out of the eight that they used it. So, from 2009, they changed it so the silver roof went to whichever driver scored the most points over ten meetings at the end of the season.

The Shootout is brilliant. I've been in it every year and I've enjoyed it every year. I've never won it, although I have come close on more than one occasion. But there's a fundamental problem. It isn't the National Points Championship and it never will be, even though the driver who wins it is given the roof colour that traditionally goes to the National Points winner, and now they've even officially labelled them the National Points Champion. It just doesn't make sense. In 2015, Dan Johnson won the silver roof after scoring the sixth-highest number of points over the season. When Ryan Harrison won in 2013, he was seventh in the grading points. In 2011, Craig Finnikin was fifth. Were they really the National Points Champion in those years?

I can see why they introduced the Shootout. It adds a bit of spice to the end of the season and keeps spectators coming through the turnstiles after the World Final. But why try to pretend that it's the National Points Championship? To me, the Shootout was a like-for-like replacement of the Grand Prix Series that we had a few years ago, but they have tried to inflate its importance by taking the roof colour from an already established competition.

Why not have both Shootout and National Points Championship? Presumably it's because the promoters don't want to pay out for two competitions, but they now have a problem of their own making. I remember saying at the time they first started messing with the National Series that it wouldn't be until a new generation of drivers starting finishing on top of the grading points and realising that they'd got nothing for it that it would become a problem. Tom Harris and Mat Newson have topped the points and have been a bit deflated when they got no recognition for it. Tom has now decided that he doesn't want to race as many meetings any more. Maybe if he saw some worth in scoring the most points over a whole season, he'd race more. The Shootout has devalued a lot of the meetings that aren't World Championship qualifiers and the like because some drivers don't see the point in going to them anymore. If driver attendance suffers then fewer fans turn up too.

If promoters had put the kind of money into the National Points that they shove into the Shootout, they'd probably have three or four drivers giving it a real go and racing hard at every meeting over the season, not just a handful. They didn't want to do that because they thought I'd win every year, but it was inevitably going to change at some point. You might say that there are twelve drivers in the Shootout and you'd never get twelve drivers in with a chance of winning the old-style National Points title, but usually you don't actually get twelve drivers actually competing in the Shootout. Most of the time, a couple of drivers don't even attempt to attend all the ten Shootout meetings, while it's clear after a meeting or two that a couple don't have the pace to win. No disrespect to them, they've done well to qualify, but they aren't going to win the silver roof.

It was most absurd in 2014 when the gap between first and second in the overall grading points was closer than first and second in the Shootout. Tom and Mat were getting really stuck in with each other but nobody was bothered, partly because nobody was told about it. All eyes were on Rob Speak instead, who ended up with an easy and slightly dull stroll to the Shootout title, despite finishing with the fourth-highest number of points that year.

I could go on, but basically it was a short-sighted decision to devalue the old National Points title and now I don't see how they can fix it. They can't just wipe the slate clean and ignore the last ten years. Anyway, I'll keep doing my best to win the Shootout. Although when I do, they'll probably change the rules again!

Ben Turner, Wainman Racing's biggest fan
of recent years

21

The UK Open weekend at Skegness is a hard couple of days. You have to dial the car in ready for one race, the second final, the one that decides the championship. I've gone well so far and I know I have the pace to finish the weekend with the championship trophy. I'm halfway through the UK Open decider and I've got into position. Now it's about finishing the thing.

I'm at the head of a train of star drivers who are exchanging blows every corner. We're an experienced crew – there's me, Paul Harrison, Rob Speak, Paul Hines and Tom Harris. We oldies are chasing down the younger drivers who started at the front of the grid: Jordan Falding, Jack Aldridge, Bradley Harrison, Joff Gibson and Michael Steward. Oh, and Rob Cowley too. Not sure he's one of the young ones!

I know the guys behind aren't going to sit back and let me slowly pull in the frontrunners. I need to make a move and I need to do it quickly. I spot a great chance and one hit with the bumper sends Joff, Joe Booth and Michael wide. In one corner I've gone from fifth to second and only Jordan Falding stands between me and a win. And I really want this one.

Jordan is a talented driver but he doesn't have the experience to drive a perfect race just yet. I move him out of the way and sprint off into the distance, never giving the other red tops a chance to get close. When the chequered flag falls I do a lap of the track with my tyres spinning, sending a cloud of smoke into the air.

I'm elated with the win. This one isn't for me, my family or my crew. It's not for my sponsors either. The sign on my roof says it all. I've been racing for Ben.

Over the last few years it had got into my head that I wasn't going to win as much. I had accepted it. I had relaxed a little bit and was enjoying it more; I wasn't getting killed at the start of every race. My plan was to keep racing, enjoying it and keep doing it as long as I can.

I've tried my best to take a step or two back from the sport, but it's just so hard to do! The only way I can stop working or thinking about stock cars is to get away completely. I've had a few holidays in Tenerife – we love it there. Just to have a few days away is fantastic. It's hard when you're self-employed and living in the same place that you work. It's hard to turn off and stop. One time, Sam managed to accidentally buy another holiday to Tenerife on Wowcher. How do you accidentally buy a holiday? She said that she was researching a trip for Phoebe and clicked to buy without meaning to! I ended up going with Sam instead. It was a three-night break and we didn't miss any racing, but just getting away from the same slog every week was brilliant. We always say that we'll have to do it again soon, then racing starts again and we don't seem to have any time.

One of the things that people often don't realise is how much stock cars can take over your life. If you are a driver who is employed in the sport too, that's even more the case. For somebody like me or Mat Newson, it's a non-stop treadmill of racing, repairing and travelling to meetings. When we get invited to weddings, we often have to miss out. Even if it is out of season, there's still plenty going on – whether it's New Zealand, the Autosport show or awards nights. There are very few dates, especially at weekends, that I have free.

Luckily I have a very understanding family. We're a tight-knit foursome – we love doing things together. Occasionally Sam and I will think about going for a meal together, only to find that the kids want to come too. That's great! Or if we want to go on holiday, they want to come too. We all enjoy each other's company.

So what is it that keeps me going and, more importantly, means that Sam is happy for me to keep racing? It's a combination of things: the buzz I get from the races, because stock car racing is a family activity we all enjoy together, and the fact that my business relies on keeping up with other drivers also plays a part. But a big part of the reason why I continue to race is because of the support that I get from the fans.

I've always had a strong following at the racetrack. I'm sure most of that came from my dad – anybody who was a fan of his naturally became a fan of me. There was a period in the 1980s when the stock car world seemed to be split into two camps, Smith and Wainman. Stuart Smith was winning everything and my dad was the best-placed driver to knock him off his perch. It meant there was a bit of extra pressure on me when I first started, but I wouldn't change that now. Ever since I first rolled on track in that all-white car, I've had a loyal following.

Right from when I was first on track, there was a Wainman fan club. Initially my mum ran it, then Sam took over when we got married. Formal fan clubs don't really exist like that anymore, but what has taken off recently is the Wainman Racing website and social media pages. When we put something good on one of those, it really takes off.

Even though we're in a digital age, we still get stuff in the post from kids. I love seeing kids' faces at meetings; they are blown away by it all. If they come and see me in the pits then I'll let them sit in the car. Sometimes I give away a trophy and I find out later that they've taken it into school and done a show and tell about it. That side of it keeps me going.

Recently, no fan has felt closer to the Wainman Racing team than Ben Turner, the boy who I dedicated the UK Open Championship to in 2015. Obviously, I want to win every race and every championship I enter, but the fact that I was doing it with 'Racing for Ben' written on my car made it more special.

Ben and his family used to come and see us in the pits and we'd chat occasionally. Then we found out that Ben had an illness, a rare form of cancer. We got more involved and tried to support the family however we could. We got to know them personally and they became friends. Ben didn't want to go to meetings because his face became disfigured and he felt vulnerable and self-conscious, but that didn't matter to us. When he realised that we wanted him involved, he did come to a few meetings. He was so upbeat about everything and so positive about his illness even though he knew he was going to die. When the end did start to come, he still wanted to know what was going on. We were even texting him results from Coventry on the night that he died – he passed away shortly after the Grand National finished.

The fact that he was the same age as Frankie really brought it home to me and connected me to Ben more than anything. It could easily have been my own son. What fifteen-year-old kid should have to plan his own funeral? But he did. After he died, his dad got in touch and told us that Ben wanted us to play a part in the funeral. His dad said that he would understand if we didn't want to be involved, but we totally did. We travelled to Derbyshire with my tarmac car for display. Ben had requested that I carry the coffin with Frankie, Danny and my dad. Then, when his coffin was lowered into the grave, Ben had asked that I fire up my car and run the engine. It was one of the hardest days I've known.

Ben absolutely loved us, right to the end. It pulled at my heartstrings; I felt raw over those few weeks. Why him? Why such a good kid? He loved life. He was salt of the earth and taken far too early. I hope I did exactly what he wanted me to at the UK Open weekend.

The UK Open win carried on a rejuvenation of my career that began with the European Championship in 2014. I went into that race pretty confident. The weekend before was a Scottish weekend road trip and I was second-quickest to Tom at Cowdenbeath and Lochgelly. I worked a little more on it during the week, just trying to find that little bit extra that might make all the difference.

Whatever I did, it worked. I arrived at Northampton for the European weekend and went out for afternoon practice where I was the quickest. That didn't go unnoticed by Tom Harris because he took the chance to smash me up in the first race. There was a big pile up on a bend and Tom followed Mat straight into me. The car was absolutely wrecked, the axles were ripped out, there was loads of steel damage and everything was out of kilter. It's a risk you take by racing the night before – if somebody considers you the main threat, they try to take you out of the running for the next day. It's certainly happened to me plenty of times before.

The team did an awesome job in helping me put the car back together but it was back to the drawing board in terms of setup. Once you lose your base settings, you lose your way. If every corner is smashed out, you don't know where you are and you have to start from scratch. But we got it back somewhere very near where it was beforehand.

I was straight out for the consolation with no wing on and ran pretty well in the Grand National, but when Norm unloaded the car the next day and had a closer look, he found that another shock absorber was slightly bent. It escaped my notice the night before because we were rushing to get back out on track. Thankfully Norm fixed it himself because at that point I was still in bed. I couldn't move! It certainly hurt. At least Tom was in the same situation with a battered body and car because Mat Newson made sure he got him back, and he did it more than once.

Come the championship race, I had a great start – I think I passed fourteen red tops on the first corner. In big races like that, I know I have to get a good start. There are too many good drivers in good cars to allow them to get away. Anyway, I laced past them all and came out behind Danny, who was running from the front of the reds. He told me afterwards that he had to double-check his mirrors when he saw me, he couldn't believe I was there already. I could tell within a straight or two that I was quicker than Danny but I tracked him for a little time until we got through the traffic.

Often I can tell how I'm going to do in a race by how I do at the start. After the first two laps of the European, I knew that I was going to get a win. After five more laps, I got past Danny for fifth place. I still had plenty of time to reel in the others in front. Despite all the damage, I had the quickest car in the race. I could see that nobody had got away. Usually in the European somebody does. Over the years, I've come second and third to yellow tops and blue tops; drivers like Paul Hines (racing a brand new car of mine) and Luke Davidson. You just don't catch them. Whenever they get away, it seems that there is never a yellow flag.

Whenever I'm winning, there is a yellow. This time, the race was stopped with three laps to go, just as I got into the lead. That's exactly what I didn't want, especially when I knew that my car was likely to go even better over the last few laps. But then I saw that the race had been stopped because Tom Harris was upside down. Actually, maybe I didn't mind the race being stopped if that's the reason!

I was first, Danny was second and Rob Speak was third. I knew that if Danny started battling me for the lead, Rob would end up winning. Thankfully, Danny seemed to agree and had the brains to settle for second. He wasn't confident that if he put me in the fence I'd stay there, or he'd have to kill his own race to do so. If he had the quicker car he probably would given it a go, but I'd won the race on that first bend, when I came out right behind Danny and surprised him. Maybe that stuck in his head a little bit.

On the day he wasn't quick enough, but we still had a Wainman one-two, which was awesome. And the way I won it – getting smashed up on Saturday night, putting it all back together and still being the quickest – it proved to me that I was still a force to be reckoned with. The European is a hard title to win from superstar, I had only won it twice before, so I was really pleased.

Having the red and yellow checks of the European Champion was great and the UK Open title meant a lot following the death of Ben Turner, but what really proved I was back on top was finishing top of the grading points in 2015 – it was the sixteenth time I'd topped the table, but the first time for six years. Young Frankie's Ministox career was coming to an end and he wasn't bothered about chasing points because he knew he'd be finishing before the end of the season, so I was able to do a few more F1 meetings and dedicate a little more time to my cars. I knew I had a chance of hanging in there in the race for points. It became clear that Rob Speak and Lee Fairhurst wanted to get the most points too, but my consistency on shale and tarmac was good all season. I won plenty of races including finals on both surfaces, and it all added up. In the end, I finished on 1090 points. Rob had 1076 and Lee had 1071. It was a really close finish (not that the promoters were interested, once again) but I was proud to get back up there.

Once more I was going to meetings and I was the one who other drivers wanted to beat. I was at the top of the sport again, after a break of a few years. Getting up there is not an easy thing to do, never mind doing it twice. But would my renaissance be a one-season wonder, or could I start another period of Wainman domination?

Tears in both our eyes after Phoebe wins
the V8 Hotstox British Championship

22

It's a wet race so I know that the first corner will be the key. I see the starter wave the green flag. The race is on.

Only I'm not in control of things – Phoebe is. She takes the first corner perfectly and the rest of the grid misses her back bumper. She started in pole position and, crucially, she has kept first place through the first corner.

I'm acting as her eyes, watching ahead, telling her what's coming up. She can't hear me, obviously, but it's almost like we have a link because she deals with every threat perfectly. It's a faultless drive from start to finish.

I'm stood on my own, arms folded, concentrating on the race, but I can feel that the eyes of the people close by are on me. With about three laps to go, somebody touches my shoulder. 'She'll be alright now,' they say.

Phoebe carries on and takes the chequered flag in the best drive of her life so far. I'm completely done in. I'm drained of all emotion. I'm supposed to be up next in the F1 British Championship, but I don't want to miss a moment of Phoebe's win. I think I'll not bother with my race.

Suddenly the pressure was on again. I was going to race meetings as the man to beat. When championships came around, I was one of the favourites. I was loving it.

I was still a busy guy. I'd spent a lot of the winter building a new shale car, although as usual I was working on it until the very last moment. I did get it done in time to win heat and final with it in the first meeting of the season, with a third in the Grand National for good measure. Considering that the only testing the car had was being driven up and down the lane at half past four in the morning on the day of the opener, I was made up with how it ran!

I had decided that I wanted to do something totally different. I got together with Clinton, my brother-in-law, and we bounced ideas off each other. He even sent me a cardboard model of what he was imagining! It was basically the body of a New Zealand superstock, but solid. I wanted to try that, but it needed a lot of work to make it fit UK rules.

One night, when I'd finished all the other work I had on and everyone else had gone home, I decided to get stuck in. I got all the loops for the cage tacked on to the chassis. By the time I was finished it was about four in the morning. The next day, I asked Danny to have a look. I value his opinion; he has an eye for these things. He walked in, looked around it, looked at me, looked at the car again... then he said, 'I can see where you're going with that. That's going to look alright.'

I built in a crease down the side panel and a back window like they have on Kiwi cars. I was going to put the bonnet inside the cage, so the cage was wider. The Chevrolet Camaro grille – a genuine part from the USA – took days to get right. Everything else had to fit around it. A few drivers had been trying the new Stuart Smith Junior-style wing, but I couldn't think of anything different to do with the wing. I didn't want to alter it just for the sake of it, although I did want to try something different. Then, late one night again, with just Adele for company in the garage (only in my headphones, unfortunately) I wondered whether it would be possible to put an extra panel inside the wing. That meant more space for signs, which is nice, and I stuck some extra flashing lights on there too.

Away from the bodywork, the chassis and the suspension were pretty much the same as the old car, although I tried jiggling the weights around a little bit to see if it made any difference. Judging by the results, it did! The cab was different though, I moved the pedals so my feet were on the floor and the steering box was inside the cab.

Aside from building my own cars, I was now looking after young Frankie's F1 too since he had made the move at the end of 2015. At least I wasn't flitting between Formula 1, V8 Hotstox and Ministox anymore. Frankie took to adult racing easily, although Sam was worried when he first started because he's a Wainman and she thought the other drivers would single him out for rough treatment. I didn't think that would happen and I've been proven right. I still look out for him though. I shouldn't, but I do. I'll have half an eye on him while I'm racing. I will him to go through gaps and watch him do stuff in my mirror.

When I first started, I certainly got singled out because I was my dad's son. Not many sons of top drivers were racing at the time, so I was seen as the new upcoming thing. People would have a go just because of my reputation. Now, times have changed. Frankie is just one of many second and third generation racers. He's also friendly and chatty in the pits; he's not big-headed and cocky. He talks to all the other drivers and always has done, and he's been given a chance to race and improve by the other drivers as a result. Of course, if he hits others, they'll hit him back, as they should. But Rob Speak said to me after a consolation at Buxton that he didn't have to move Frankie, he moved aside at the right time, but then he was right back on Rob's back bumper following him round. That's him learning what he's doing.

Frankie's first chance in a major championship was at the 2016 British at Skegness. By that time he was already a red top after winning a few races from white at the end of the season before, but he knew that he shouldn't overreach so was just aiming to qualify for the championship race. He just managed it – a sixth place got him onto the last slot on the grid. A third, fourth and sixth was good enough for me too. I would start on the outside of the third row. That was pretty good, considering that my engine only got put back in the car the evening before. I finished up at four in the morning on the day of the championship – probably not ideal preparation.

Part of the reason why everything was so last minute was because Phoebe was also racing in the V8 Hotstox British Championship so there was an extra car to prepare. And she was flying! She raced in two heats, winning the first and finishing second in the other, which put her on pole position in the championship race. When that happened, I had to step aside a little bit and look after her. She was panicking. She had never started a big race on pole, so wanted to clarify exactly what to do. She also had Adam Joyce behind her – he can be a bit of a hard hitter, he'll put the bumper in on anything in sight, so we were both a bit nervous. Phoebe asked what she should do. I talked her through the rolling lap, psychologically preparing her for the fact that she might go out of the race on the first corner. That can happen – if they had got to her, they would do her. I told her to look in her mirrors going into the first corner. If she thought they were going to dive-bomb her, I told her to go deep and let them go with her. If she controlled it, she would come out first. If they were not going to get to her, I told her to go in dead slow. They would all charge past her backside like idiots and she would be off.

Her nerves can't have been helped when it started raining as they were gridding up. She came back to the pits and we changed a tyre, then she went back out and controlled the rolling lap perfectly. She checked her mirrors into the first corner, saw that they were going to miss her, and did a cool, tight turn. The car looked like it was a remote control one. To drive like that, when it was wet, was the best she has ever driven.

I charged down to the finish line and gave Phoebe a huge hug when she got out of the car. We were both really emotional. After the celebrations I returned to the pits, but I felt quite empty – Phoebe's win had drained me. I wasn't bothered about my own championship race, but I knew that I needed to get ready and try to get in the right headspace for a full-contact bumperfest. I was starting on the outside of the track, so I knew I'd be in the middle of all the action.

As expected, I got taken out at the start. I hit the fence on the first lap and Colin Goodswen climbed over the front of my car. Little Frankie almost got taken out too, I saw him just avoid the tyres through Colin's window! When the yellow flags were waved, I was at the back with twenty-odd cars lined up in front of me. I remember looking at the left front shock absorber during the stoppage. It was damaged where Colin had hit me. I said to myself, well, at least Phoebe won.

I came so close to pulling off. I had a damaged car and I was way down the grid. But then I looked at the front and I could see Ryan Harrison, Lee Fairhurst and Rob Speak. I knew it was going to kick off. I thought if I kept going I might get past a few and still get a top ten finish.

After the restart, despite the damage, the car was on rails. I worked my way through and ended up back near the fight for the lead. Once I was up to fifth or sixth, I knew I was in with a shot. Lee put Ryan in, then Ryan put Lee in, and I went for Ryan.

The result of the dogfight was that Danny and Mat Newson got past for first and second. At that stage, Danny should have won it. He should have nailed Mat straight away, but instead spent a few laps faffing around which gave me a chance to catch up again. It's a championship, get on with it! Danny eventually put Mat up the wall and I got past too, but I was more clinical. The next bend, I put Danny on the wet outside line and got through on the inside. You've got to do it straight away. I knew Danny's car was slightly damaged because he had hit the wall early on, so I was confident he wouldn't be able to get me back. Then I came round and saw the board showing three laps left. Hang on, this could actually happen! Phoebe jumped back into my head – I'd forgotten in the adrenaline rush of the race, but now I had time to think.

When I passed the chequered flag, I was in a state of shock. It was a bit of a blur. I didn't do any donuts, I just parked up on the home straight and sat there. I had won the British Championship on the same day that my daughter had won her version. My brother had finished second. At one stage, we thought Frankie was going for third too, although we later found out he was a lap down. It was amazing. Nothing like that will ever happen again, will it? Some good things happen in life and that was one of them. I'd have taken Phoebe's win on its own, that was good enough for me. Her win certainly meant more to me.

I was made up with the British title, it was the eighth time I'd won it. I've made that title my own almost as much as I have the grading points. I finished top of that list again in 2016 – the seventeenth time – and picked up the Grand National Championship too. What I didn't expect, because I've learned not to expect it anymore, was to win the World Final.

The 2016 World Final had some similarities to 1998 and 2005. Just like 2005, I knew I had the car to win it – we were racing at Coventry and the new shale car was awesome there all season. Because of that, winning the British and topping the points from early on, I think I was probably the pre-race favourite.

The day itself was spoiled by the rain. Everyone was saying that I'd enjoy it because of the weather, but I didn't want it wet. It's a big weekend for fans, sponsors and drivers; the showpiece event of our sport, so you don't want it lashing down. But it's true that I know how to drive in the wet. The track was just right considering the conditions, my car was right, and the setup was right. I'd timed it to get away early. Over the years, I've worked out how to manage my car so it'll still be quick over the closing laps despite a setup favouring the start. Rob Speak, who was probably my biggest threat, had gone the other way – he set up for a good finish.

The outside of the second row can be a bit of a dodgy place to start. I had to be careful going down the home straight. If the cars behind you are coming quick, you're in the fence, you can't do anything about it. I hung out wide to see what was going on and spotted a gap to get on the inside going into the first turn. Rob put Nigel Green around the fence and followed him into it, which let me and Mat Newson through. Then Mat crashed into a parked car and I nearly crashed into Mat, but I managed to get up the inside and over the kerb.

That led to a lot of moaning after the race, just like the first time I won the World Final in 1998. But it was either crash into Mat or go over the kerb. What are you supposed to do? I know what the moaners would say – crash into Mat – but that's only because they want to see me out of the race. When you're sideways going into a corner and there is a car in front of you, you can't suddenly turn 180 degrees the wrong way and go around the outside. It was the same when I hit Chris Cowley. Chris had spun in front of me, I had committed to the corner. I couldn't get inside him, couldn't get outside, so I took the hit and made sure I hit him dead straight so I didn't damage anything. I shot over the kerb in the impact, but it was only about thirty feet. Watch Paul Harrison and he goes the length of the straight on the middle. Dan Johnson and Mick Sworder dived over the middle then too; Rob Speak even passed Sworder over the middle.

As always with World Finals, I had to cope with more than one lot of yellow flags, but every time the race stopped, I made sure that I got away well on the restart. You regroup and go again. The hardest part for me was letting Dan Johnson get away when he got into the lead. I was in second place and I had to let him go. It's quite a hard thing to do, but I knew that Dan always cooks his tyres and I could keep them in better condition. I don't floor it. You can spin your tyres right down the straight every lap if you want, but I can feel if it's breaking traction. The car won't go any faster like that, so don't do it. But you try telling yourself that in the World Final while Dan is spinning his tyres and pulling away from you! What if I got it wrong and I just let him drive away for the title? It was hard, trust me.

I had to force myself to drive conservatively. It got to a point where he stopped pulling away, then he started coming back towards me. I got right on top of him and had just decided how I was going to deal with him. I was going to stick him in the crap on the outside line which would have given me plenty of time to get through and get away without putting him out of the race. I'd have liked him to get second. But then he caught a Dutch car and popped his right front tyre. I saw it straight away, so did he, and he moved out of my way.

I checked my mirror when the five-lap board came out. Rob Speak was in second, but quite a way back. Everybody knew it was Rob's last season before retirement and I'd heard all sorts of rumours that he was going to take me out. Was he going to dive over the middle and crash into me? I was confident that he wouldn't do anything silly like that. Rob and I have had plenty of hits over the years, but he's a racer, not a crasher. He would never have done anything like that – although some of his team would probably have wanted him to. After the race, he was pleased with second place, but some of them had faces like thunder.

I got a bit excited towards the end and went into the pits bend a bit too fast on a couple of laps. I had to have a word with myself. I just needed to drive like I had in the rest of the race. I settled down and circulated to the chequered flag. This time I did do donuts, at either end of the track. If the British Championship left me drained, after this one I was elated. The first person I saw was Norm. He was chuffed as nuts. Phoebe got to present me with the trophy, that was nice, and Frankie and Sam both congratulated me, but it wasn't a huge family moment. Phoebe had to work the rest of the meeting, Frankie had more races to come, Sam was soon back in the restaurant with her buddies. I knew that we'd all catch up later.

I don't think I watched a race after the World Final because we had to strip the car for post-race scrutineering. We got it in the secure compound and they told us to take off all four shockers so they could put them on the dynamometer, all four brake pads had to come out, all four wheels came off. Then we put the car in the back of the truck because they wanted the gearbox and bell housing out, you can't do mine from the top so we put it in the truck to get underneath it and lifted it up. I wasn't bothered. If they want to check something they're going to find a way to do it, there's no point in getting irate. They can't check everything but the stuff that could have been messed about with, they did check.

I tried to spend as much time as possible with the fans too. Some have been with me for a lot of years and stuck with me through thick and thin, so I wanted to see as many of them as I could – it was their night too. But there's only so much time, so the World Masters meeting the day after is the best time to celebrate. Doing a parade lap as World Champion there is the best time to acknowledge the fans and get recognition for everybody involved in the win; the team, family and sponsors. It was important to have a gold wing for the next day, but I only had about twelve hours to get one. Craig from Premier Motorsport Developments had a spare wing, but it was silver! What was I supposed to do with that? I rang Karl Hawkins and told him to buy a load of gold paint. He asked who was going to paint the wing, and I told him that he was!

At least I had the next few days to get the wings properly sorted. Both tarmac and shale wings were sent up and down the country to be painted, glittered and signwritten. It costs a fortune, but it's got to be done. If you're going to be the World Champion, you have to do it right. I turned up at Stoke with a fully complete gold wing and everybody told me that it looked brilliant. Comments like that made me feel ten feet tall.

Was 2016 my best ever season? Probably not, but it wasn't far off. I had won more races and more finals in other seasons, but the way the sport is changing, nobody wins dozens of finals in a season anymore. It just doesn't happen. I won thirty-one races and nine finals – the drivers with the next-highest numbers of final wins had four. The year before, I finished top of the grading points by fourteen points. This time, the gap was 386.

Not every season is as good. I wanted to do well in 2017, the year which would mark my thirtieth in Formula 1 stock car racing, but I started a little off the pace. I wasn't dreadful, but I certainly wasn't dominating like I had the year before. Sometimes it's because you have a new car to bed in, but I was struggling on shale and I was using the same car that had been so good the year before. It hadn't had any major work done, it wasn't stripped over the winter, it was just repainted and had a little refurb. Eventually we discovered after a couple of months that there was a brake problem. Over the winter we had swapped one of the front stub ends which had been modified for the bigger discs but we hadn't realised that one of the brake pads was hooking onto the steel part of the fabrication and not pressing on the disc properly. It was throwing the balance of the car but, not realising the problem, we were altering the setup which made things even worse.

We eventually caught it and fixed the problem the weekend before the British Championship – ideal timing! I travelled to Sheffield feeling a little more confident, and that confidence increased when I finished second in the first heat. The key to a good British campaign is consistent finishes, so I was happy enough with seventh in my second heat. My last heat was the final one and I'd worked out that the best grid position I could get was the outside of the second row, but then it chucked it down with rain and I realised that the outside of the track would be a quagmire. I got into the lead, but it was an unusual situation. I didn't want to win the race because it would give me a bad grid position in the championship. Going into a corner, I overcooked it and spun, allowing Dan Johnson and Stuart Smith Junior past, meaning that I finished third and started the main race on the inside of the third row. Did I spin on purpose? No comment!

It stopped raining and the track staff did their best, but it was a mess for the championship race – the outside rows had no chance. Dan Johnson, Tom Harris and me charged off into the first three places before Tom put Dan into the fence, letting Tom into first place and me into second. Then, when Tom came to lap Dan, it all slowed down. Most people assume that Dan was braking deliberately to slow Tom, but Dan says that he thought we were under caution. I don't know what happened with him, but I can tell you that I thought we were under waved yellows. When Dan slowed, Tom slowed behind him and barely touched him. Then a backmarker slowed too. I came up to the three slow-moving cars and assumed that we had waved yellows, so I became the fourth car in a slow train. We followed each other for a third of a lap until I spotted a car parked in the fence with a static yellow flag by it. That's when I realised that we weren't under caution, so I put my foot to the floor, got past the backmarker and hit Tom into Dan. Only then were the yellow flags actually waved.

I was fortunate that I'd been able to catch Tom, but now I had another problem. My clutch had gone. I had to do the rolling lap in first gear and change into second when the green flag was waved without the clutch, by feathering the revs. Had Tom known, he could have just dabbed his brake before the green flag and I'd have stalled. Instead Tom went as normal, but he still built a good lead because I had to be careful with my gear change. Tom could have run away with the race then, but luckily he came back to me when he clipped Mark Gilbank.

That got me within touching distance and gave me a chance. I made my decision. It's Sheffield – you don't pass cars cleanly there, you have to put them away. I gave Tom a hell of a hit and just managed to avoid his car as it bounced out of the fence. Credit to Tom – I didn't expect him to keep going, but he did and managed to finish sixth. There was no maliciousness in the move, but I had one chance and had to take it. He'd have done exactly the same thing – in fact, he told me so after the race!

That brought my total to nine British Championships, another trophy to add to my collection. Over the course of thirty years, I've won the silver roof thirteen times and topped the points on seventeen occasions. I've been World Champion three times and European Champion

three times. I've won the New Zealand 240 Champion-
ship three times. In the Netherlands, I've won the World
Cup three times and the Long Track Championship once.
Not to mention the Grand National Championship,
Grand Prix Series, UK Open, World of Shale and Scot-
tish Championship.

It's quite a list, and one I've not finished with yet.

Two of the best drivers I've had the pleasure to race against – I'd have won loads more titles if it wasn't for them!

23

What will stock car racing be like in ten years time? This is my vision:

The reconstructed Coventry Motorsport Arena is full to capacity with 20,000 fans watching me win a ninth World Final, breaking the record held by John Lund for so long. I've been racing for forty years and the last decade has been one of my best. I've won the silver roof multiple times, helped by the fact that it has been given back to the person who wins the most points over the season. I've made it to ten British Championship titles. And I've won the British World Final, Dutch World Cup and New Zealand World 240 Championship in the same calendar year.

I pass the chequered flag and the fireworks go off. I spin the car at each end of the track, clouds of shale and tyre smoke mixing in the sky above the arena. Then I go and park by the *podium alongside the other cars in the top three: the 555 car belonging to Frankie and the 211 car belonging to Phoebe. Maybe next year, I'll let one of them win. On second thoughts, maybe not!*

I think that I'm the greatest stock car driver of all time. There, I said it.

I'm sure that many people will consider me some kind of madman just for saying that. It's often seen as some kind of undeniable truth that Stuart Smith is the best driver the sport has ever known. Let's just check the statistics. We've both won the silver roof thirteen times. Yes, he won the World Final five times to my three, but I also topped the grading points on another four occasions without winning the silver roof. Yes, he won 500 finals to my 275 or so, but I have won the British Championship nine times to his three. He won 1,611 races, but I have won more than 1,100 and that doesn't include many wins in the Netherlands and New Zealand, never mind the Long Track Championship, three World Cups and three World 240 titles to my name.

Basically, I think it's a lot closer than many people might think. If we were able to time travel so I could race against Stuart Smith in identical cars when we were both in our prime, I honestly don't know who would win – but there wouldn't be a lot in it.

The trouble is that it's difficult, some might say impossible, to compare eras. Back in the sixties, seventies and eighties, lower graders were there to make the numbers up. Now, especially on tarmac, you have good drivers with very good cars in white, yellow and blue grade. When you look on MyLaps they are just as quick as me and the other superstars, but they only have to pass three cars or whatever and they are at the front. I start eight and a half seconds back and have thirty cars to pass. It's never going to happen.

It's partly my own fault that I've had to race against drivers with similar cars, sometimes even better cars, than I was in. For years I've been churning out decent stock cars at a reasonable price. Now, with a few other car builders contributing too, it means that every driver is capable of buying a competitive car. Whether they drive a Wainman, Harris, Falding, Newson or whatever, they'll have a good car to drive. They're all fundamentally similar. Nobody is a step ahead when it comes to the chassis, the only way some drivers try to get an advantage nowadays is to buy an expensive American engine and rev the life out of it.

One of the other all-time greats is John Lund. He was the best driver of his time, but not of all time. He dominated just after Stuart retired and before I took over. Certainly when I came into the sport, John was top dog. I started racing at the end of 1987, a season in which he won his first World Final, British Championship and National Points title. He'd waited ages for a big win then three came along at once! To win the three biggest titles in UK stock car racing in the same season is a phenomenal achievement, and a sign of how John was dominant at that time. The only other drivers to win the treble are Stuart Smith, Ellis Ford and me.

Because John was the main man when I first started, I made a point of doing my best to knock him off his perch. He was always the one I aimed to beat, even if it meant being a bit rougher with him than with everybody else. It was a plan with two benefits: first, I might actually beat him; second, even if that didn't work, it sent a signal to all the other drivers that I wasn't somebody to be messed with. I was on my way to the top. By the mid-nineties, I think I had the measure of John, although there's no doubt he was still my number one opponent. At the turn of the millennium, particularly after he missed a lot of racing due to the foot-and-mouth disease outbreak, he began to drop off the pace a bit.

If I targeted John on purpose because I wanted to take out the top driver, I've also been on the receiving end. Most obviously, that happened when Rob Speak moved into Formula 1. He wanted to send a signal of intent and the best way to do that was to have a go at me. It showed that he had no fear, but just like John, I wasn't willing to back down without a fight. That led to some big hits, most notably at Wimbledon, but it continued right through both of Rob's spells in F1 including during his last season.

Many people think that I chased Rob out of F1 the first time he quit, but that's not true. There's a relationship that me and Rob have that many people don't see. From our days in Ministox, we had a healthy respect for each other. That continued when we raced separately in F1 and F2 and carried on when we were coming together after Rob started in F1. He was a threat coming in because he had a bit of money backing him and he certainly had the talent, but he didn't have the right cars to start with. When I built him a car, he went out and won the European Championship in it. I wouldn't have built him a car like that if I didn't get on with him.

Yes, there were some heated moments featuring 515 and 318. Rob is probably the hardest driver I've driven against. Not only can he dish it out, he can take it too. Maybe that's why we clashed on the track, because I'm the same. Rob came straight over to me after his last ever race at Coventry and shook my hand. He told me that it had been pleasure to race against me. And I think it has been a pleasure to race against Rob.

Rob seemed really happy to stop the second time he announced he was leaving F1. He is his own man and doesn't need people trying to pull strings for him. The National Points Shootout in 2016 is a good example. In my opinion, Tom Harris was there to help Rob by taking out his opposition, but Rob was perfectly capable of winning without any help. If he was going to take the title, I wanted him to do it on his own. It made me lose my temper a bit, so I made sure that Tom didn't qualify for the final. I didn't want him to start interfering with the championship because I expected him to try and have a dive at Nigel Green. By that point I knew that I knew that I wasn't going to win but I wanted to make sure that whoever did win really deserved it. I could have qualified for the final and taken Speaky out, but it wouldn't have been right – but I think Tom would have taken out other cars to help Rob.

All great stock car drivers have respect for other drivers, it's how the job works, but I don't think that Tom Harris has much respect for the others out there. It's all about him. If there was one moment when my relationship with Tom crumbled, it was after the Theo van Lier incident in the Netherlands. I didn't like that at all. I was right there and helped to pull Theo out of the car and it really affected me. I'm not saying I won't ever trust Tom again, but he'll have to work to get my respect and trust back, and at the moment he's not doing anything to do that.

If there's one name that my stock car career will always be linked to, it's Andy Smith. He was one of the best; a very, very good driver. I don't really know why he stopped, whether he was hurting physically or mentally after the death of his dad, but I do think it's a shame he's not still racing. He had the ability, the know-how and the track craft to do it, he had respect for other drivers, and he used it to win an awful lot of championships and races. He never won a European Championship, but that's his own fault – he should never have let slip that he wanted to, because after that I made sure he didn't win one!

The rivalry between me and Andy developed just at a period when we were both going really well and sharing most of the major titles between us. Every World Final saw us starting on the front row together, every World Final was about which of us would win (usually him!), and it all happened just as the BBC cameras were there to capture it all, which magnified the rivalry off the track. I don't think we'll ever be best friends, but I am proud to have shared one of the finest periods of Formula 1 history with him.

All in all, I've raced against hundreds of different drivers at dozens of different tracks over three different decades. Every single person who has rolled out on track has contributed to making Formula 1 stock cars what it is today, in however small a way. I like to think that I've played a bigger part than most. I've won a heck of a lot. I've built more cars than I can count. I counted up recently and I reckon I've competed at more than 1,500 stock car meetings. I know that, whenever I finish racing, people will never be able to talk about me without mentioning stock cars. I've spent so much of my life racing, building, talking and thinking about stock cars. And you know what? There's nothing I'd rather have done.

During my third stint as World Champion – but I wouldn't have won a single title without the help of many different people

ACKNOWLEDGEMENTS

This book is sub-titled My Life in Stock Cars, but it really should be My Life IS Stock Cars! Yet it's impossible for one person to race stock cars alone – it takes an entire team of people just to get out on track, never mind to be successful and run a business too.

Over thirty years, I've had loads of different people help me out on the cars, both in the workshop and in the pits. Currently my crew includes Richard 'Norm' Brighton, Dan 'Denby' Mitchell, Chris Binns, Esmond Cloxton and Raz. Some of my previous mechanics include Richard Thornton, Ian Frobisher, Kevin Offord, Paul and Ian Minto, Guy Parker and my stepfather, Brian Woodrup. I'm also indebted to Martin O'Neill for his help and the long hours he put in during my Ministox career.

I think that everybody knows that stock car drivers often have to sacrifice a lot of time to compete on the track, but what people often overlook is the sacrifices that the mechanics make too. The time that they spend with me in the workshop or at the track is time that they could have spent with their family or doing other things. So, thanks to all the mechanics who have helped the 515 cars to pass the chequered flag, both now and in the past.

I think I can build a pretty decent car, but the engine that powers it isn't really my thing. For twenty or so years, I've relied on Ian Whitworth to build those for me. He has powered me to many race and championship wins.

Stock car racing is expensive, despite it being a working man's sport. I've already mentioned Tim Mann and Tony Cole, who provided sponsorship during the 1990s when I really needed a leg up to be competitive. But I've had many other sponsors over the years, too many to thank individually. Currently, I'm sponsored by Bensons Oils, Marie Curie, AHT Logistics, Tony Goodsir Commercial Engineers, Wainman Static Caravans, Castle Tyres, Hopkins Construction, MAB Contractors, Sam Betts and CA Betts, Startrax, Blythewood Plant Hire, DEB Teesdale, Teng Tools, Lockhart Plant Hire, AKA Paintwork, Jason Holden Car Repairs, Graham Edwards Trailers, Brian Evans Signs, Ralph 01, Lucas Oils, Silksworth Aquatics, Evolve Branding, Wez-tec, Firow Propshafts, Premier Motorsport Developments, Mintex and TMR. Some of my sponsors developed into long-term relationships. For many years I was sponsored by GTR Refrigeration. When George and Jane gave up that business, they continued to help me out – now I have the name of their granddaughter, Amaia Jane, on my car instead!

I've also been privileged to have had the opportunity to race around the world. I've crossed the English Channel countless times and the number of trips I've made to New Zealand is well into double figures. But there's no way I'd have been able to race on the other side of the world so many times without the backing of Stan and Sonja Hickey, who have provided race cars, storage, advice and friendship to me and Sam since 1995.

The stock car world is like one big family. What other form of motorsport has drivers helping out their opponents in the pits, trying to repair their car so they can get back on track and compete again? Just like every family, there are occasional squabbles and fall outs. I've been involved in my fair share of those, but I like to think it has usually stayed on the track. I respect each and every one of the thousands of drivers I've competed against since my debut in Ministox in the early 1980s.

I decided to write this book because I thought that my fans would be keen to know a little more about me and my life stock car racing. I hope you've enjoyed it! Scott Reeves helped me put my thoughts and memories on paper, while Carl Hesketh and Gary Reeves were proofreaders. Rob Speak wasn't just an excellent driver and opponent on the track, he has provided an excellent foreword.

A fire at the farm and a flood at my mum's house means that I don't have very many photographs from the early part of my stock car career. So thanks to the photographers who have provided the pictures that illustrate this book: Dave Bastock, Colin Casserley, Mike Greenwood, Martin Fitzgerald and Paul Tully.

I have to thank my family. The support I get from them is invaluable. I love the fact that stock car racing is something that we've all done as a family: Granddad, Grandma and Mum were crucial to my early career. My dad was also a massive influence and a great help. Although we had a bit of a falling out at the start of my F1 career, we cleared the air and I spent many happy years racing with him. Since Dad retired, I've been joined on track by my brother. Danny and I might travel to meetings separately, but we're still really close. Now I get to race alongside my kids. I'm so glad that Phoebe and Frankie enjoy racing just as much as their old man.

And let's not forget Sam. She's the crew chief who keeps everything running smoothly. She doesn't mind when I come to bed in the early hours because I've been working in the garage and she's my number 1 fan on the terraces. Imagine what life would have been like if I hadn't spent my life building, repairing and racing stock cars? I bet she'd have hated it!

Winning the World Final in 2017 –
hopefully not my last gold roof win

CAREER ACHIEVEMENTS

as at July 2017

World Champion: 1998, 2005, 2016
National Points Champion: 1994, 1996, 1997, 1998, 1999, 2000, 2001, 2002, 2003, 2004, 2005, 2007, 2008
British Champion: 1992, 1999, 2001, 2003, 2004, 2005, 2006, 2016, 2017
European Champion: 1995, 2006, 2014

World Long Track Champion: 1998
World Cup winner: 1999, 2006, 2015
World 240 Champion: 1997, 2000, 2009

UK Open Champion: 2001, 2003, 2006, 2009, 2015
Grand National Champion: 1995, 1997, 2000, 2001, 2002, 2003, 2004, 2005, 2011, 2014, 2016
Trust Fund Champion: 1991, 1998, 2002, 2004
Scottish Champion: 2000, 2001, 2002, 2003, 2004, 2005
BriSCA Supreme Champion: 1991, 1993, 2010
Grand Prix Champion: 1998
Bumper Trophy winner: 1990, 2001, 2004, 2006
World of Shale Champion: 1999, 2001, 2012
Dutch Open Champion: 1990, 1992

Race wins: 1135
Finals wins: 275

KINGS OF THE OVAL

by Scott Reeves

Sixty years on from its birth in 1954, Formula 1 stock cars remains the premier oval motorsport. Unlimited horsepower propels the cars around the track, but speed isn't everything – contact is expected and encouraged. It takes a huge amount of bravery to win in this brutal arena.

Jump behind the wheel with nine F1 stock car champions – find out what drives them to success, how they deal their rivals and what motivates them to risk everything in pursuit of the chequered flag.

Kings of the Oval combines their honest accounts with over 100 photographs from the sixtieth season and rich history of the formula.

My Time

by Paul Harrison

"I just feel that my time has come."

When Paul Harrison uttered those words before the Formula 1 Stock Car World Final in 2011, he was about to make history. It was the culmination of a life spent trying to match his father's achievement and wear the gold roof that signifies the World Champion.

Paul Harrison tells the story of his year as World Champion, revealing the determination and willpower that is required to remain at the top of stock car racing. From the exhilaration of victory to the pressure of performing under the gold roof, *My Time* is a unique behind-the-scenes account of this brutal motorsport.

Also from Chequered Flag Publishing

KEEP TURNING LEFT

by Scott Reeves

Success in the world of Formula 2 stock car racing takes a rare combination of aggression, skill and luck. Only the best drivers get to race under the gold roof of the World Champion.

In *Keep Turning Left*, twelve top F2 drivers give an open and honest account of racing bumper to bumper in full contact motorsport. They reveal their highs and lows, their motivations and frustrations, their joys and regrets.

With over 100 colour photographs and intimate access to the drivers, this is a must-read book for every follower of Formula 2 stock car racing.

Also from Chequered Flag Publishing

GOLD TOP
The John Lund Story

by Scott Reeves

In 1987, John Lund's eleven year struggle behind the wheel finally came good – he won the stock car World Final. Little did he realise that over twenty years later he would still be part of the sport, having won the World Final more times than any other.

Gold Top tells the story behind John Lund's stock car career. Based on interviews with John and his family, it draws the rich anecdotes from a quiet and modest champion to conjure a colourful and compelling biography.

From triumph to tragedy, this is the long journey that made John Lund one of the most experienced, popular and successful drivers in the history of motorsport.

Also from Chequered Flag Publishing:

F1stockcars.com
Season Review
2016

2016 – the year when Wainman and Speak battled for supremacy and the Coventry Stadium saga dominated the headlines.

The *F1stockcars.com Season Review 2016* contains the best content from the biggest Formula 1 stock car fan website, with new and never-before-seen feature articles.

Profits from the sale of this book will be donated to the BSCDA Trust Fund.

INNOVATIVE AND EXCITING SPORTS BOOKS

Chequered Flag
PUBLISHING

www.chequeredflagpublishing.co.uk

CPSIA information can be obtained
at www.ICGtesting.com
Printed in the USA
BVOW06s1727100118
504981BV00008B/58/P